# THE LABYRINTH OF POSSIBILITY

T0347381

# THE LABYRINTH OF POSSIBILITY
## A Therapeutic Factor in Analytical Practice

*Giorgio Tricarico*

Translated by Lisa McCreadie

Routledge
Taylor & Francis Group

LONDON AND NEW YORK

First published in Italian in 2009 as *Daidalon—L'archetipo della possibilitá nella pratica analitica* by Moretti & Vitali Editori

First published 2015 by
Karnac Books Ltd.

Published 2018 by Routledge
2 Park Square, Milton Park, Abingdon, Oxon OX14 4RN
711 Third Avenue, New York, NY 10017, USA

*Routledge is an imprint of the Taylor & Francis Group, an informa business*

British Library Cataloguing in Publication Data

A C.I.P. for this book is available from the British Library

ISBN-13: 9781782201762 (pbk)

Typeset by V Publishing Solutions Pvt Ltd., Chennai, India

*To Kata-Riina, my Anima,*
*to Joonas Lennon and Nooa Aaron, Wonderful Possibilities*
*and to my Bears*

# CONTENTS

ACKNOWLEDGEMENTS                                                ix

ABOUT THE AUTHOR                                                xi

FOREWORD                                                       xiii
*Donald E. Kalsched*

PREFACE TO THE ITALIAN EDITION                                 xix

PREFACE TO THE ENGLISH EDITION                                 xxv

PART I: MAIN THEME

*CHAPTER ONE*
Tuning—questions                                                 3

*CHAPTER TWO*
First tunes—the labyrinth between archaeology, etymology,
   and symbology                                                11

*CHAPTER THREE*
Main theme—Possibility                                          21

PART II: CHORUS

*CHAPTER FOUR*
Main verses—Possibility, right to existence, and ego complex    35

*CHAPTER FIVE*
Chorus—possible comparisons                                     49

PART III: MIDDLE-EIGHT

*CHAPTER SIX*
Theory and ethics                                               63

PART IV: DEVELOPMENT AND CLOSING CHORDS

*CHAPTER SEVEN*
Developing the theme—Possibility, Impossibility,
  and individuation                                             67

*CHAPTER EIGHT*
Closing chords—Possibility and Limit                            85

*CONCLUSION*
Suspended cadence                                               99

*NOTES*                                                         101

*REFERENCES*                                                    109

*INDEX*                                                         113

# ACKNOWLEDGEMENTS

I am grateful to all the people who chose me, as their analyst, to walk along a meaningful part of their life-path.

I am grateful to Eva Pattis and Carla Stroppa, without whom this book would not have existed, and to Enrico Moretti at Moretti & Vitali, for the trust and the possibility to publish this book in Italy, in 2009.

I am grateful to Donald Kalsched and Sonu Shamdasani for their precious help and warm support.

I am grateful to the people who read, commented on, or in various ways inspired this book in its English translation: Günther Anders, Sergio Buccheri, Jeffrey Scott Buckley, Renato Cattaneo, Susanne Eberhard Petersen, David Evans, Wolfgang Giegerich, Aksel Haaning, Hilary Hahn, George Harrison, Polly Jean Harvey, Paul Hewson, Richard Hogan, Astri Hognestad, Hans Jonas, Carl Gustav Jung, Verena Kast, Tia Kuchmy, Bodil Kulseng, John Lennon, Virginija Liveikienė, Paola Livorsi, Monika Luik, Aili Maar, Paul McCartney, Gunilla Midboe, Steven Patrick Morrissey, Natalia Pavlikova, Ursula Peterson, Ebe Pöder, Heidi Reiljan, Inger Safvestad, Signe Sammelselg, Konstantin Slepak, Richard Starkey, Ulla Olin-Stridh, Bente Thygesen,

Pirjo Tuovila, Pille Varmann, Joan Wasser, Margaret Wilkinson, Thom Yorke, Luigi Zoja, and Luisa Zoppi.

I am grateful to Lisa McCreadie, translator of this book from Italian to English, for her patience, her curiosity, her cleverness, and her commitment.

I am very grateful to Constance Govindin, Kate Pearce, Oliver Rathbone, Alyson Silverwood, Rod Tweedy, and all the people at Karnac Books, for their unique way to be altogether very professional, helpful, and kind.

## ABOUT THE AUTHOR

**Giorgio Tricarico**, born in Milan, Italy, in 1970, is a clinical psychologist and a Jungian analyst member of the International Association for Analytical Psychology. He has worked with adult patients since 1998, and has given several lectures and seminars on relevant issues in Analytical Psychology. Since 2009, he has been living and working in Helsinki, Finland, as a psychologist, psychotherapist, and Jungian analyst. Writer of essays and short stories, he is also a singer and guitarist, active since 1990 in many projects and bands.

# FOREWORD

*Donald E. Kalsched*

This is an optimistic book by an original new voice on the psychoanalytic scene. In this book, Giorgio Tricarico adds his voice to those of us who, like Jung, emphasise the prospective, teleological elements in the human psyche, our inherent longings for a full realisation of the potentials latent in the self, emergent around the constellating impact of important relationships in the interpersonal environment.

For the author, one of the most important of these "constellating impacts" in analysis is the emergence of what he calls the "archetype of Possibility". This occurs within the patient, but is directly dependent upon the relationship with the analyst. Sometimes the most subtle factors in the analyst's attitude can constellate a *sense of possibility* in a patient, following a supervisory session, for example, during which the analyst's view of his or her patient is expanded, and then, miraculously, the therapy suddenly moves forward. Or a slight re-framing of the patient's impossibly negative assumptions as containing a kernel of something good, can constellate the "archetype of Possibility" and bring new meaning to the analytic adventure and a sense that a path forward exists (as in the case of Laika, pp. 6–8).

The author is hopeful that his model of psychotherapy, built around constellation of the "archetype of Possibility", might prove to be a universal factor present when a therapeutic relationship is effective.

By labelling this therapeutic factor the *archetype* of Possibility, the author wants to emphasise the transformative inner factor that always "strives" for life, for meaning, and for integration and wholeness.

This striving comes from *within* as an inherent potential in the human personality. It is "constellated", or not, through relationship, including by the earliest attachment relationships in the child's life within which ego development evolves. Borrowing a phrase from Verena Kast that is relevant to the very earliest moments of the child's subjectivity and ego development, Tricarico underscores how the infant is *authorised to exist* by another subject:

> The subjectivity of the child begins to emerge in the relationship with the subjectivity by which he/she feels authorized to exist because he/she is loved. The paradox is that the child already exists but does not know it. It is not the caregiver who gives him something that he/she does not have. However, the child, unconsciously, needs a subject to allow him/her to feel that he/she *can* exist.

Feeling "able to exist" after such *authorisation* is equivalent, the author suggests, to the constellation of the archetype of Possibility which already exists in the unconscious as a "potential ego"—a predisposition to develop consciousness.

> The child with no name, no identity, feels both being attributed to him by the people taking care of him and *discovers being, after feeling that he can be and before knowing who he is.*

The authorisation or entitlement to *be* a *subject* (as opposed to being an object in the (m)other's mind) is, in the author's understanding, not something many of our patients can take for granted given their early attachment derailments, relational trauma, and the subsequent operation of intractable defences that have ironically "come to their rescue" in the never-ending struggle for survival.

Speaking to these defences, the author has been impressed by the fact that many people who come for analysis describe their situation as "feeling stuck and going nowhere", or "going in circles", or feeling imprisoned, blocked, thwarted, or "being at a dead-end" in life with no way out, that is, no freedom, no meaningful direction to life, no possibility of a path forward.

He realised that the image of the labyrinth (or *daídalon*, from the mythic architect of the labyrinth, Daedalus) was an ancient and universally evocative out-picturing of this condition, with its curvilinear meanderings and its two roads, leading to "death", on the one hand, or to renewed life, on the other. He further realised that a journey into the labyrinth always contains the *possibility* of renewal because the road "in" can also be the road "out", if the Ariadnine thread of possibility can be constellated and followed by the patient into a renewed sense of aliveness.

Having done his anthropological research on the consensual significance of the classical labyrinth, or *daídalon*, Tricarico (following mainly Kerényi) highlights the dominant interpretation of the image as referring to a ritual journey into the "underworld", the realm of Spirit and the world of the dead, seeking a relationship between the world of the dead and the world of the living—a relationship crucial to early humans. In this view, the meandering journey through the labyrinth represents the "cycle of life–death–rebirth and eternity". Its ritual repetition would thus put the initiate into an intimate relationship with these great mysteries and their cultural meaning.

Following Jung, it is a short step from this understanding to a symbolic grasp of the image as the psychological descent into the unconscious in search of the "treasure" of the feminine soul (Ariadne) hidden there and menaced by the marauding Minotaur, as, for example, in the story of Theseus. Tricarico accepts these rich symbolic interpretations but does not linger there.

Beyond the anthropological or the symbolic interpretations of the labyrinth, Tricarico adds a third crucial element, one that aligns his ideas with my own on psychological defences and their archetypal nature (see Kalsched, 1996, 2012). He suggests that the labyrinth might not just stand for "the unconscious" into which the analytic journey must be undertaken in order to recover "lost" potentials, but may also represent the imprisoning enclave of defences that fills the patient's psyche with negative assumptions about life's *impossibility*.

He acknowledges that these defences, with their corrosive negative "voices", become addictive, often leading to the negative therapeutic reaction, and to painful "failed" cases. He also admits that many patients unconsciously resist leaving their familiar, yet torturous, sanctuary/prisons, and may spend most of their lives severely limited by such defensive traps. He insists, nonetheless, that the potential always remains for a glimpse of the "possibility" of a way out of these defensive spirals.

In this acknowledgement of *impossibility*, and the fact that the labyrinth sometimes wins in the struggle to free the patient, Tricarico acknowledges what I have elsewhere called the "self-care system" of defence (Kalsched, 1996, 2012), a structure necessitated by dissociation, occupied by an innocent remainder of the whole self (Ariadne) and its inner persecutor (the Minotaur).

Thus, the labyrinth is a defence "designed" by a mysterious architect in the psyche to vouchsafe the patient's traumatically wounded innocence while at the same time, tragically, re-traumatising this core of selfhood and keeping it demoralised in order to keep it from risking the possibilities of life, possibilities that the "system" has found unbearably painful in the past. In the process, the innocent core of the patient undergoes a de-evolution, and what might be a benign regression becomes a malignant one. As I have detailed in earlier work, the defensive system thus operates in a fashion exactly analogous to auto-immune disease in the body, attacking healthy tissue in order to replicate itself and "survive" as a system, at the expense of the overall health of the patient.

In agreement with Tricarico, I have emphasised that giving up this labyrinth of survival defences is always a possibility, because it is not the original condition but a secondary defensive one. I have also emphasised that this possibility depends almost entirely on whether early relational trauma can be re-worked in the patient's relational life later, beginning with the attachment relationship in the transference/countertransference. I have described how this negotiation is likely to be a very stormy one, involving a life-or-death battle between the possibilities for true life glimpsed by the patient and the convictions of impossibility represented by the defences. How this battle comes out depends to a frightening degree upon the analytic partners' willingness to open to both the love and hate that are mobilised in the struggle. With enough faith and devotion, the archetype of Possibility may be glimpsed by both participants and then, as the author admits in the context of an especially challenging case, the analyst may be "greatly moved and get goosebumps" (p. 43).

By embracing the psyche's potential for self-realisation and the life-quickening effect of relationship on the activation of our full possibilities as humans, Giorgio Tricarico places himself squarely in the tradition of some of my favourite writers and mentors, including Jung. One such is Martin Buber, whose essays on philosophical anthropology fell into my hands when I was a twenty-five-year-old beginning psychotherapist. These essays, published in 1965 and titled *The Knowledge of Man: A Philosophy of the Interhuman*, contain some of the most inspirational ideas I have encountered on the general subject of how one's life can be "authorised" by another person, Tricarico's equivalent to the constellation of the "archetype of Possibility".

I wish to conclude these remarks with the beautiful words of Buber himself:

> A man cannot really be grasped except on the basis of the gift of the spirit which belongs to man alone among all things, the spirit as sharing decisively in the personal life of the living [human being] …
> To be aware of a man, therefore, means in particular to perceive his wholeness as a person determined by the spirit; it means to perceive the dynamic centre which stamps his every utterance, action, and attitude with the recognizable sign of uniqueness …
>
> If we want to do today's work and prepare tomorrow's with clear sight, then we must develop in ourselves and in the next generation a gift which lives in man's inwardness as a Cinderella, one day to be a princess. Some call it intuition, … I prefer the name "imagining the real" for in its essential being this gift is not a looking at the other but a bold swinging … into the life of the other … in his wholeness, unity, and uniqueness, and with his dynamic centre which realizes all these things ever anew …
>
> (pp. 80–81)

> Man wishes to be confirmed in his being by man, and wishes to have a presence in the being of the other. The human person needs confirmation because man as man needs it. An animal does not need to be confirmed, for it is what it is unquestionably. It is different with man: Sent forth from the natural domain of species into the hazard of the solitary category, surrounded by the air of a chaos which came into being with him, secretly and bashfully he watches

for a Yes which allows him to be and which can come to him only from one human person to another. It is from one man to another that the heavenly bread of self-being is passed.

(p. 71)

*Donald E. Kalsched, PhD*
*Newfoundland, Canada*

# PREFACE TO THE ITALIAN EDITION

A *heartfelt* book needs someone to bring it to life.

From a rational perspective, this book could be considered a collection of the insights and reflections I have developed throughout my early years in clinical practice, but that would not fully correspond to my experience.

More accurately, those insights and reflections emerged, slowly but surely, from some deep, dark depths of a world parallel to conscious reality, revolving in particular around a symbolic interpretation of the image of the labyrinth.

To paraphrase Jung when he wrote about autonomous complexes, I do not think it was so much that I had the inspiration to write these pages. It was inspiration which *had me*.

To back up this unusual impression, in March 2005 I had a dream, of which I remember only this brief glimpse:

> I am in a room of colleagues, other analysts, students and teachers of the Jungian school to which I belong. I am explaining my theory on the labyrinth to them. "It is a way of working of the mind/ psyche" [sic], I declare. I set out the various passages of what I will write and the ideas taken from my experience with my patients …

As is often the case, the clarity of the ideas, the perfect coherence of the statements, as well as the natural flow of the reasoning, had completely vanished, evaporated, when I awoke from that dream.

When I began the laborious task of putting something down on paper, more than four months had passed and I was, along with my partner, in Lahti, enjoying the end of the Finnish summer.

I alternated between extensive reading and bursts of writing. For the former, I sought out *my* places—immersed in the silence of the forest or sitting at a table in a beautiful wooden cafe, which was once a small train station, on the banks of the great lake Vesijärvi. For the latter, the quiet of the tiny apartment we lived in.

But what I wrote rarely came close to the purity of the ideas expressed in that short dream in March.

At any rate, from then onwards, many other insights took shape, and further reflections were added, breathing life into the pages of the present work.

This book's primary purpose is to propose a model that aims to capture what happens between analyst and patient when a therapeutic relationship is effective. I have often been struck by the phrase "it is the relationship that heals" in a course of therapy, regardless of which school the therapist belongs to and his theoretical/clinical, and therefore technical, background. But I've always been unsatisfied with this statement, however true.

In search of an answer to help to clarify what happens in daily practice with my patients, I will outline a hypothetical model of a therapeutic factor using analytical psychology as a vertex of observation. I do so with the deep-rooted conviction that this is a place of rich and substantial knowledge, heuristically useful for a profound understanding of the psyche.

The first part of the book unfolds in a chronological fashion. It outlines a series of observations and insights that have led to the emergence of the subject in question, via analysis of the image of the labyrinth from historical, mythological, and, above all, symbolic, points of view. In that first exploratory phase, valuable support was offered by a collection of essays by Károly Kerényi, the famous scholar of mythology and historian of religions, who, a little less than seventy years ago, published a text on mythology with Carl Gustav Jung. Based on the many visions that the symbol of the labyrinth brings to mind, I will offer an unsaturated interpretation as an "archetypal image", which could be originated by an archetype of Possibility, in Jungian terms.

When dealing with the concept of archetype, in all its complexity and controversy, it seemed important to consider its epistemological significance. This involved taking into consideration both the criticisms and the mythologising to which it has been subjected throughout the history of analytical psychology, in order to clarify how the concept would be understood in this book.

In the second part, what Jung might call "constellation of the archetype of Possibility" within a course of therapy and formation of the ego complex (or emergence of consciousness from the unconscious) are placed side by side. Apparently different theories of the mind, however far removed from one another, share a common denominator in terms of observing what happens between patient and therapist, if we consider this in light of the hypothesis described. A look at some of the cases I have encountered in my clinical experience and that of other colleagues, Jungians and those belonging to different schools of thought, will give evidence to the latter statement.

The third part is probably the shortest ever written, consisting of just two phrases which came to me of their own accord in as many moments over the autumn of 2006. As these phrases were the result of unconscious reflection, I decided to simply put them down on paper without developing them any further, as for a dream or an image.

In the fourth and final part, the topics of negative therapeutic reaction, the death instinct, and the concept of a defensive Self are covered.

Talking about Possibility necessarily unearths a confrontation in all those situations in which it seems impossible to make progress towards "healing". This latter term could be deemed rather narrow and ill-suited to the purpose of describing analysis, as it is linked to the corresponding medical concept, and more generally associated with the operating model that characterises the so-called society of technology.

Bearing in mind the concept of individuation, the ultimate purpose of human existence promoted by the Self, according to Jung, here it is proposed the archetype of Possibility be considered as a "bridge" between the Self and the emergence of the ego complex. Thus, the start of the individuation process would be marked not by confrontation of the ego with the contents of the unconscious but by the birth of the ego itself and the origin of consciousness.

This may represent a possible rapprochement between Jungian theory and clinical theories developed by relational depth psychologies, which deal with the ups and downs of the emerging consciousness more systematically than the approach favoured by Jung.

This point in particular took shape of its own accord during the writing process, shifting its course more than I could have imagined at the start.

The book ends with a collection of reflections on possibility, impossibility, and limit in modern Western culture as, in order to fully grasp the essence of the psyche, the reality by which we are surrounded must be taken into consideration just as much as our "inner landscape", that ever-changing, infinite inner world which belongs to us and to which we belong.

It is important to clear up any misunderstandings over the concept of Possibility: unlike the common use of this term, which often has omnipotent connotations (as in the expression "anything is possible"), Possibility is intrinsically linked to the dimension of *risk*, and is not remotely equivalent to *certainty*, nor to the denial of the Limit.

Indeed, there can be Possibility only in a dialectical confrontation with the Limit, which may thereby determine the greater or lesser probability. In total contrast with the simplistic "positive thinking" of so much current psychology, which risks nurturing the general attitude of repression of the Limit, speaking about Possibility requires a genuine confrontation with the risk of failure and with Impossibility itself.

Since the image of the labyrinth has a tremendous power of attraction and could trap in its meanders thoughts that deserve broader horizons, it is important to gradually let it fade into the background and instead keep in the foreground the concept of Possibility.

The conceptual framework expressed in the present work is expertly summarised by Jung, as he wrote the following on psychology:

> It is not a question of his *asserting* anything, but of constructing a *model* which opens up a promising and useful field of inquiry. A model does not assert that something *is* so, it simply illustrates a particular mode of observation.

> (Jung, 1947/1954, p. 184)

Being well aware of the impossibility of an objective psychology (given that each discussion *on the psyche* is inevitably a discussion *of the psyche* of the author), the ultimate aim of this work is thus to propose a model from which reflection on what happens in therapy can move forward (*transgredior*, in Latin to break/to infringe, from which derives the English word "transgressor"; etymologically, it means "to go beyond"). I do hope that this happens in the most useful possible way, which is being able to ask further questions.

# PREFACE TO THE ENGLISH EDITION

*Möglichkeit*, "possibility", is the word at which C. G. Jung's *Liber Novus* is left interrupted, but I could not have known this, as the *Red Book* was published in October 2009, some seven months later than the first, Italian edition of my book.

I wrote the first complete draft of my manuscript during a difficult period of my life, essentially between December 2006 and August 2007, reworking my intermediate thesis, which dated back to a couple of years earlier. Being still immersed in my analytical training, a more critical attitude towards Jung's ideas was impossible, at that time, as I still had to grasp them and explore them from their inside.

Working on the English edition of my book, I often wondered to myself whether I should have changed something in the text, updating it to where I am now, as a person and as an analyst.

Several books have left something important in my soul, several experiences have brought me somewhere else, in the last seven years. Shouldn't I have integrated deeper reflections on the nature of archetypes, in the light of books such as, for instance, Jean Knox's *Archetype, Attachment, Analysis*? Shouldn't I have filtered some parts of my work through the lenses of Wolfgang Giegerich's challenging developments of C. G. Jung's theory? And what about the work of several different authors on the therapeutic factors in analysis?

Apart from some slight but meaningful changes suggested by Sonu Shamdasani, who kindly read my manuscript and commented on it, I decided to leave the manuscript basically unaltered, with its ideas expressed as they were in the Italian edition, even with its naiveté, at times.

The perception of unconscious possibilities within a meaningful relationship as a therapeutic factor in analysis, the reflections on the concept of possibility itself, the idea that our theories can define what is possible and what is not, are still alive ideas, present in my clinical practice. Although questionable, these ideas could at least invite other therapists to make their own frame of meaning explicit, and this seemed to me a good reason not to change anything.

At the present moment, immersed in the issue of the quest for meaning after the end of meaning, reflecting on *Möglichkeit*, Possibility seems to me the junction between Existence and Essence, as written in the conclusion of my book, or, in other words, between the *opus parvum* of my clinical practice and the *opus magnum* of our opening to the Soul.

*Giorgio Tricarico*
*Helsinki*

# PART I

## MAIN THEME

## CHAPTER ONE

# Tuning—questions

One of the first things you must practise, when learning to play the guitar, is tuning. Long before I had started to consider exploring the psyche, and thanks to my father, I embraced this instrument—physically too, because as you play the guitar sitting down, you embrace it.

When tuning the guitar, you have to start from just one note, a "La" ("A", in English) and from this practice was born the expression "*dare il La*" in Italian (literally, to give an "A"), meaning a starting point, an *incipit*, the beginning of something. In the study of the psyche, the "La" triggering reflections is often clinical experience with the patients themselves.

Even this work had a "La"; actually two, to be precise. The first line of enquiry arose from a frequent observation in psychotherapy, one that may plausibly have occurred to anyone involved in this work: when dealing with a case, it often happens that situations that seem to represent a serious obstacle, a core problem, a point at which the therapy has clearly run aground, actually turn out to be extremely important, even useful, to the therapy process or helpful in progressing towards change, if cultivated and exploited.

For example, in the session following a supervision, sometimes the therapist simply having gained a different view of what is happening can be somehow "perceived" by the patient and, most importantly, this leads to some form of progress, so the situation is diffused and progresses in a new direction.

I was particularly struck by this notion. And yet I should have known that something of this nature had already happened, as I had read extensively on the subject, on the history of analytical thinking, right from its beginnings.

At the end of the nineteenth century, for example, the delusions and hallucinations of schizophrenics and psychotics were seen as meaningless events, fruit of the mysterious malfunctioning of a weak and sick mind. But when we began to treat them as having sense/meaning, significant changes were seen in certain patients.

C. G. Jung was amongst the first to see a meaning in the delusional symptoms of what at the time was known as *dementia praecox*, as is reflected in *The Content of the Psychoses* (Jung, 1908/1914). About this work, Frey-Rohn speaks aptly of "a new approach to psychotherapy", in which "instead of dismissing the systematized fantasies of demented persons as bizarre and nothing more, [Jung] found it more appropriate to arouse in the patient a feeling that his fantastic formations had a meaning common to all humans" (Frey-Rohn, 1990, p. 78).

Even the idea of the neurotic symptom as a failed attempt at healing, developed by Jung throughout the evolution of his thinking, and the prospective view of disorders, associated with this idea, are further examples of new ways of looking at a mental subject. These ways pioneered a new direction in the approach to the patient's discomfort and often saw changes deep within the patients themselves. A different perception of the clinical situation on the part of the therapist, somehow picked up on by the patient, clears the way for new horizons in the therapy process, opens new ways. But why?

Let's leave this question for a moment and move on to the second "La". The second observation that led to further questions and considerations is that our mind, in order to visualise how certain phenomena unfold, tends to make use of metaphors of movement within a horizontal space.

With regard to psychotherapy, spatial metaphors are without a doubt the form of expression *par excellence*, used by both the patient and the therapist. Significantly, the therapy itself is often called a *journey*.

The common feelings of many patients dealing with psychic discomfort are described with expressions such as: *finding oneself at a dead end*, in a *bottomless pit*, in a situation with *no way out*; lost, disorientated, like being in Dante's dark forest, a meaningful representation of the psychic condition of the poet at the beginning of his inner journey.

The sense of searching for something implicit in the idea of a therapeutic journey (search for greater balance, understanding, meaning, integration, thinkability, transformation, individuation) is often expressed with images linked to a horizontal spatial representation, as can be seen in use of expressions such as *taking steps forward*, rather than *backwards, finding oneself at a crossroads, exploring* one's own story, *crossing a bridge, going in circles, looking for a way out, a door, treading new ground, a new path, charting a course, finding oneself back at square one*, and so on.

There are also images that refer to movements on a vertical axis, such as fluctuating between *highs and lows*, aiming to *cheer up, feeling down, picking oneself up*.

These expressions seem to be linked to the positive connotation associated with reaching a higher point, as if recalling what happened in terms of phylogenetics in the evolutionary process which led to standing upright, use of the hands, and, consequently, considerable development of the brain—a process that every human being reflects throughout their own lives starting from birth.

Finally, in reference to vertical movement, patients and analysts make use of images related to going *into the depths*, to the *core*, to the *heart*; expressions that, unlike the previous ones, imply a negative connotation to remaining on the surface.

At any rate, the horizontal spatial metaphor seems to be the most commonly used, omnipresent in references and publications about psychology, psychoanalysis, and psychotherapy, and it is along this dimension that these psychological theories produce explanatory principles which translate, perforce, into a method.

In fact, *hodos* in Greek means "road" and *metà* means "beyond". Therefore, "method", the *metà-hodos*, can be defined as a road (to be travelled) which goes beyond, which leads to new scenarios and opens up broader horizons.

One of the best concepts to effectively express what an analyst tries to do with the patient during sessions is "opening up *meaning*", where the last word in Italian, "*senso*", also refers to *direction* (the same happens with German "*sinn*"). Opening up means imparting "sense" (meaning plus direction) to the unique and personal stories of our individual lives, as is also the case with the still short history of psychology, of a little over one hundred years.

*  *  *

I saw Laika for a period of almost four years in a rather flexible setting, due to her work and the fact that she came from a far-off city.

She had shown two very distinctive traits during therapy. The first was the way she talked: in a loud voice and an agitated manner, always accompanied by effusive gestures and non-verbal emphasis. The second was that she took up almost the entire duration of the session with her story, leaving me with only the last five minutes to express what I felt or thought (the reason why with her I was rarely able to restrict the session to fifty minutes).

Another peculiar trait of her therapeutic journey was its cyclical nature. First there was a series of positive sessions in which important aspects initiating a dialogue between conscious and unconscious would emerge. Laika herself experienced new situations in reality and started behaving more constructively (being fully aware of this herself, moreover), on cue. But along would come a session in which nothing that she had done was of any value.

In her words, my efforts to help her were in vain; she was worth nothing; she had never learned anything; time was passing by relentlessly and her life was always unhappy, whilst other people could live so much better than her as they created far fewer problems for themselves; who knew how long she would have to come to therapy with me, and so on.

In these situations, my (sometimes ill-concealed) countertransferal reaction was of deep anger. Other times, however, I felt the same disappointment as Laika and a deep sense of uselessness and powerlessness.

Thinking back on it now, the image of a child comes to mind, who, after painstakingly and carefully building a sandcastle on the seashore, methodically destroys it and then despairs. It truly seemed, to use a spatial metaphor of my own, like a situation with no way out.

Valuable support, in theoretical terms, was offered by reading Jung's complex theory and also an interesting book by Donald Kalsched, which we will cover later. Instead of standing helplessly by when faced with her destructive behaviour, I tried to ask myself what meaning this could have.

I had begun to feel that when the patient was feeling this way, she seemed very similar to the ward sister she worked under at the hospital, and of whom she often spoke: this sister was described as hypercritical, able to breed ill-feeling among colleagues, biased, terribly jealous, destructive, and in hindsight, not very good at her job. I took to calling this person whom I found in front of me, cyclically, after a few useful sessions, the "inner sister", and to say it, in the same terms, to the patient as well.

When Laika arrived with the unmistakeable attitude of destruction and belittlement of the work that she herself, up until the previous session, had recognised as useful, I said "Ah, today we have our inner sister as well" and pulled up a chair next to the one she was sitting in to accommodate "the other one". (I had never used this practice before and have never used it since, not with Laika or with any other patient, but with a very concrete patient, as she was during that phase of therapy, it turned out to be much more useful than a metaphor.)

In addition to this visible act, I started to hint that probably this "inner sister" wanted to tell us something when she turned up, and that she should be listened to somehow. In other words, we should have tried to get in touch with her together and engage her in what we were doing.

In the next session, the patient came with a dream—a rather rare and unexpected occurrence for her. In the dream, she was in a very distressing situation. Someone in the family was dying or had already died, and the rest of the patient's family (father, mother, other people) were behaving as if nothing was happening, ignoring the gravity of what was going on, to her great dismay. She started to shout furious abuse at everyone for their indifference and, running to a phone box, disconsolate, she would call her ward sister (the same despised sister!) to tell her what was happening. The patient's surprise when faced with this dream situation was great.

Without delving any deeper into the interpretation of this dream (for which we would need a more detailed history and the patient's associations), I would like to highlight how it showed that she *could* interact with the "inner sister" and not only suffer her ill-effects. In fact, not only could she interact with her but, in a painful and distressing situation, it was this very person, so unpleasant in real life, who seemed to be of help and comfort, in total contrast with what the patient might consciously have thought.

The interesting point for the purposes of our discussion is that when the factor that seemed to be standing in the way of the therapeutic process was viewed as something that perhaps was not simply blindly destructive but rather useful, even if in a way that was not altogether clear, we were able to *take a step forward*, and thus *get out of a vicious circle* in which the patient herself suffered greatly.

After that session, Laika still brought out her destructive side but much less frequently than before, and moreover, an important channel (or to stick with the spatial metaphors, one could also say "a path") to work on was opened up.

The ever-critical and deprecating attitude of the real ward sister was discovered to be very similar to that of Laika's mother, as well as being a characteristic of that part of herself that we had dubbed the "inner sister". In Jungian terms, the dialogue between the ego complex and a negative mother complex (a dialogue initiated by the phone call in the dream) represented the beginning of a *possible path*, which led, towards the end of therapy, to greater collaboration between the parts.

I remember fondly the time when, in one of our last sessions, Laika genuinely acknowledged having faced many difficulties in her life and having done so many things, though she was feeling very bad, including painstakingly carving out a space for therapy for herself. "I have been really good", she said, with modest firmness—a phrase that was no longer being attacked by the "inner sister". This, in fact, seemed to have become useful for protecting Laika from people in the external world who were, in various ways, dangerous, and thus was being put to a much healthier use.

By presenting certain aspects of this case, we can highlight the opening up of meaning that came about when some potential and usefulness was seen in something that seemed to be nothing but damaging and useless. A *possible path* materialised before us, where previously there had been only a sterile and cyclical vacuum.

* * *

The question we left aside a few pages ago ("why a different perception of the situation on the part of the therapist, which the patient has some-how picked up on, *opens new paths* in the therapeutic process?"), and the contemporary view of the natural use of spatial metaphors, continually brought to mind an image that had never interested me previously: the image of the labyrinth.

Being lost and looking for a path, finding yourself in blind alleys, retracing your steps, finding yourself back at square one, great anxiety and confusion, these typical expressions of the psychic process in therapy all seemed to me simultaneously related to the experience of being in a labyrinth.

As with the action of an automatic reflex, the mere word immediately evoked other images, such as the Greek myth of Theseus, the palace of Minos, the Minotaur, Ariadne, and her famous thread.

But what does the symbol of the labyrinth refer to? What does it reveal, *beyond* the myth, by which I mean even "before" the Greek myth that has immortalised it?

What happened during the period when this question was prowling along my mind is interesting. By chance, when scanning the bibliography at the end of a book I was reading, I was struck by the title of a collection of papers by Kerényi, the same Kàroly Kerényi who had collaborated with Jung, peremptorily entitled *In the Labyrinth*.

So, led by the hand by the many reflections contained in that collection and with the help of other authors who wrote on the subject, I delved into the passages on the symbol of the labyrinth and its various interpretations, to finally emerge with a clinical hypothesis.

The tuning was finished.

The playing could begin.

## CHAPTER TWO

# First tunes—the labyrinth between archaeology, etymology, and symbology

As a Jungian, I could probably begin with a detailed analytical presentation of the myth of Theseus, knowing that mythical tale is the living expression of the reality of the Soul and thus of inestimable value to a psychologist, who should deal with the Soul itself. But this has already definitely been analysed from every possible point of view (literary, historical, linguistic, archaeological, and even symbolical).

For the purposes of this work, thus, let us leave the famous mythological tale aside, with its characters, their feats, and their possible interpretations, and instead look to explore the meanderings, as it were, which make up the symbol of the labyrinth itself, in search of visions, as Hillman stated,[1] and other suggestions made long ago.

A symbol signifies nothing.

"Signi-fy" means "to do a sign, to make a sign", and so when a symbol signi-fies something, it is dead, it has been killed, it has been forever silenced. If the labyrinth is a symbol, it cannot signi-fy anything but rather can "refer to", "evoke", and "allude to" in a fascinating, numinous, and ultimately mysterious way.

At any rate, exploring what the labyrinth refers to should begin on the island of Crete, to pay homage to the place most closely linked to the *daídalon*. The island of Crete has been inhabited for at least eight thousand years, in the centre of a Mediterranean that was then starting to become a place of travel and contacts, with its Knossos, that hub of Minoan civilisation, whose beginnings date back to approximately 2400 BC. The adjective "Minoan" clearly derives from the name of the mythical King Minos which ancient historians used to denote a particular person they believed had really existed, but which today is thought to have been the name given to sovereigns in general.

The nineteenth century, with its renewed interest in archaeology, saw numerous excavation missions on the island, searching for traces of pre-Hellenic civilisation. It was the Englishman Arthur Evans who left his mark with the discovery of a grand, intricately mapped building, which initially confirmed the existence of a palace-labyrinth built around 1900 BC and abandoned approximately six hundred years later (Brown, 1994).

The case of Evans and the residence of King Minos is currently one of the least accredited. The architectural aspects characterising the edifice (the poorly lit rooms and the long, dark corridors winding around a large inner courtyard) do not seem to suggest a strictly residential purpose but argue more in favour of a building for religious or ritual purposes, perhaps related to bull sacrifices—a sacred and emblematic animal in Minoan-Cretan civilisation.

Four centuries before Evans, one Cristoforo Buondelmonti became interested in the Cretan *daídalon*, although he did not travel to Knossos but rather to the cave excavations in Gortyna, identifying these as the mythical labyrinth.

In the Classical Era, the theory that the labyrinth was an extraordinary building created by the architectural genius Daedalus was widely believed, although its exact location was not known even to ancient mythographers, who sometimes referred to Knossos and its palace and sometimes, on the other hand, to Gortyna and its caves.

Kerényi himself reports that "a first historical evidence about Minotaur's cavern dates back the 4th century; close to Gortyna, in the terrirory of the mythical kingdom of Minos, a stone cave underground is shown to the travellers as the famous labyrinth" (Kerényi, 1983, p. 55; translated for this edition). The connection between the caves in Gortyna and the labyrinth could be found in the etymological root of the word *labyrinthos*, which can be linked to the word *labrys*, indicating a certain type of double-edged axe in Greek, also depicted in the decoration on the walls of the rooms of the palace at Knossos. The *labrys* was the tool used to construct the *labyrinthos*, which can be consequently defined as a "stone cave, a mine with many wells, caves and cavities" (ibid.).

It appears that the tools of ancient miners, in this form, were also depicted in the tunnels, now empty, of the Cave of the Sibyl at Cumae, another place that was recognised, of old, as a "labyrinth". In fact, according to the myth, the architect Daedalus, fleeing on his wings from Crete, was saved at Cumae, and on the door of the sanctuary he had drawn a map of the Cretan labyrinth. Even Virgil, in the *Aeneid*, gives a detailed description of it, by setting Aeneas off on his journey to the Kingdom of the Dead from that very place.

Also on the subject of *labrys*, Kerényi notes that in a group of monuments in a mining area in the south of France, a certain type of axe used by miners was found which, in Roman times, also appeared as a recurring theme in sepulchral symbology. The same kind of double-edged axe is depicted hanging above two columns in an image of a sarcophagus in Agia Triada, an area in the south-west of Knossos, featuring a ritual being performed by two priestesses.

In light of these references, we can conclude that the *labrys* was definitely an implement used in caves but, in all probability, was also a ritual tool. Fragments of the complex vision on which we are trying to shed light—the labyrinth, the caverns, the caves, the double-edged axe, the underground mines and the natural cavities in the earth—seem to be united by one thread of meaning. This could be represented by the descent to the Underworld, the journey to the Realm of the Dead, followed by a return to life and by rituals related to death and rebirth.

Etymological references allow us to delve into language as one would dig to find the dregs of the human experience. In this speleology of meaning, we strike concretions of forgotten sounds, artefacts buried in words that we still use today, the original meaning of which speaks quietly and gives rise to numerous assumptions accompanied by emotions, a real imaginal activity.

As the dominant chord in the subject in question, the etymological theory of the word *labyrinth* favoured by Kerényi is not the only one. In Herodotus, where the term was first used, it meant "tomb or place of the ancestors".[2] The "father of history" picked up the word in Egypt, visiting the inaccessible tombs of the kings and using it in the original meaning of *"Penates"*. In reference to this other piece of linguistic sediment too, however, we still find ourselves in that detached and dark place where those who lived and died before us dwell.

As an archaic symbol linked to ritual practices, the labyrinth was originally represented in a meandering curvilinear shape, which only in subsequent eras was replaced by the form of angular meanders, or the shape that we commonly recognise as the labyrinth. This older image (also called the "classical labyrinth") appears on the sides of certain Cretan coins, as well as in the decoration of ceilings, doorways, and walls of the palaces of Knossos. But it can still be found also in many other cities, such as Tiryns, for example, and on the burial mounds of Mycenae, as well as those in Egypt. In fact, it can be found at the most diverse of latitudes, over a large variety of cultures and peoples: in tattoo designs of the indigenous peoples of New Zealand and on the doorways of their places of worship, as well as in the decoration found on wood and stones in central Australia, and on models for tattoos all over southern India.

On the Old Continent, classical labyrinths can be found in Norway, Iceland, England, and Wales, as well as over a large area of Central Europe, from Belgium and Germany to Hungary and the Balkan region. In Scandinavia, the meandering curvilinear labyrinth design often takes the shape of low constructions made of stone, and is mainly built in two ways: in one, the path is unicursal and has no dead ends; while the other, at a certain point in the passage, reaches a fork where one branch

Figure 1. Classical labyrinth.

leads to a dead end and the other leads to the exit. This design brings to mind, amongst others, a theme typical of many stories—that of the two roads, where one, usually taken by the hero, is apparently simple but is actually fraught with near-insurmountable difficulties, whilst the other, taken by secondary characters, is safer but not conclusive.

Present at certain famous sites of cave paintings (Bohuslän, Val Camonica, Pontevedra), as well as at the Neolithic monuments on the island of Malta and in pre-dynastic Egypt, the image of the labyrinth really seems to belong to the heritage of mankind from the oldest Neolithic and Megalithic cultures.

The dominant interpretation is that this is not a mere ornamental design or simple decoration but a depiction of a tortuous journey which, with its convolutions, alluded to the cycle of life–death–rebirth and eternity. The same presence of the fork in the road could be related to the idea that death actually has two possible outcomes, one negative and one positive, with a return to life.[3]

The link between images of the classical labyrinth in the very distant cultures in which these appear thus seems to be the representation of the world of the spirit or the Realm of the Dead, places separated from the world of the living but with which it is possible to have dialogue through specific rituals.

The unsettling core of meaning at the heart of these historical, archaeological, and etymological amplifications is that of travelling a road which allows you to turn away from death to renewed life.

This becomes even more evident as we return to the pages of Kerényi's work, where he maintains so decisively that all research on the labyrinth must necessarily take root in dance. Drawing an interesting parallel between the figure of Persephone (Queen of the Underworld, in spite of herself, who, according to the myth was destined to spend four months per year in the Realm of the Dead in the company of Hades and the other eight months on earth, with her mother Demetra) and the figure of a girl who was the protagonist of a series of Indonesian tales, Kerényi opens up other visions of the symbol in question.

As Eleusis, near Athens, celebrated Persephone's return from the Realm of the Dead, in Indonesia a divine event took place every year: the Moon Goddess, Hainuwele or Rabie, was kidnapped by the Sun God. Curiously, the ritual does not consist of depiction of the kidnap, but of a particular dance reproducing the form of the classical labyrinth, the so-called *Maro* dance. In this dance, men trace out a line of nine spirals making up a meandering curvilinear labyrinth, by dancing it, in the centre of which is a girl. (This is similar to the rituals performed inside the labyrinth forms in Scandinavia, where men would dance along the curves, whilst in the centre sat a virgin. Among Swedish-speaking Finnish people, in fact, this type of dance is called *Jungfrudans*, the "dance of the virgin".[4])

The Indonesian *Maro* dance seems to be closely linked to a represen-tation of a journey to the Realm of the Dead, and it is not the only exam-ple of this kind of dance. In the New Hebrides, for example, dances depicting images of the classical labyrinth linked to representation of a journey to the Underworld are performed with the wish to renew one's own life through contact with dead ancestors. All these dances aim to express the possibility of rebirth after walking "into death", to then re-emerge into the light.

A labyrinth dance is also mentioned in *The Iliad*, without being directly defined as such. Homer speaks of the dancing place that Daedalus had built in Knossos for Ariadne. From Homer, we also learn that the legendary shield of Achilles, forged and decorated by the god Hephaestus, featured boys and girls dancing, joined at the wrists, in a long procession that changed direction at a certain point at the first dancers. The effect produced by this type of choreography is that one row begins to dance in front of another, with an inversion of movement which creates convolutions.

In the famous myth of Theseus, we are told of a dance that the hero performs after killing the Minotaur, along with all the other freed hos-tages. He is said to have imitated the journey he made through the labyrinth *in dance*, and Theseus is said to have learned this dance from Daedalus himself. This was to celebrate being free from the danger of death—salvation—and according to certain versions of the myth, Theseus did this dance on the island of Delos.

The Greek name for the dance performed by Theseus is "*geranos*", or "dance of the crane". The crane dancers are drawn into the dance by the "*geranulkos*", or "he who drives the crane", who guides the procession of dancers who, in turn, hold in their hands a rope, representing the thread of Ariadne. In this type of dance, too, like in the labyrinth dances and in the one depicted on the shield of *Peleus Achilles*, the direction is inverted at a certain point and convolutions are created. Initially, it is danced towards the centre (into the labyrinth, towards death), after which the dance changes direction towards the outside (the return to the light, rebirth).[5] The rope, as the symbolic element referring to the mythical thread of Ariadne and therefore to salvation from the labyrinth of Knossos, seems to have a definite meaning. But why were these dances defined as "in the manner of the crane"? What could the reference to a bird indicate?

Kerényi reckons the reason behind the name of this type of dance could lie with a chorus of *Hippolytus* by Euripides. The chorus, made up of a group of women, declares its wish to disappear "into giant caverns", but the Greek word could also be translated as "in the shadow of the clouds". Sky and cave are in some way related, connected by a common etymological root and, according to Kerényi, it is as if these women wished to transform into birds to be able to escape. This transformation would take place in giant caverns. In this image, the author sees a reference to the cave, and therefore to the *labrys*, to the Underworld, crossing the threshold to the afterlife to then be reborn to a new life.

Kerényi states that:

> caves and birds are linked by a semantic connection, the same one that links labyrinth and cranes: this connection explains perfectly the reason why Daedalus, both builder and prisoner in the labyrinth, knew only two means to escape to freedom from his fatal construction: the thread and the flight.
>
> (Kerényi, 1983, p. 65; translated for this edition)

Daedalus taught love-struck Ariadne how to use the thread to save Theseus, while he himself experimented with flight later, along with his hapless son Icarus, to escape the labyrinth in which Minos had shut him as punishment. The "crane dance" would thus express the idea of the return from death, the idea of transformation and salvation.[6]

As underground caves, tunnels, and caverns are the "labyrinth" forms that can be found in nature, so the labyrinth, danced, carved onto tablets, painted, portrayed through mosaics, or built on stone walls, is the form created by man to express, according to Kerényi, the continuation of life after death.[7]

Our vision of the labyrinth has expanded to include dance, the artistic form of expression which most radically needs to be embodied, as it is brought to life by movement of the human body. Dance and the labyrinth—movement of the body and the unmoving rigidity of stone arranged into passages—seem to be opposites which, in the tale we are piecing together, are interwoven, in dialogue, making reference to each other.

The metaphor of music that accompanies us in the chapters of this book takes on a particular significance when it refers to the unknown form of music that must have accompanied these ancient dances. The lost harmonies that rent the air during the ritual dance and which bewitched the senses of those dancing human beings in the convolutions of the labyrinth can only be mute assumptions to our ears. We must content ourselves with the harmony of images that emerges from references to the symbol we are dealing with, which, in dance, powerfully evoked the possibility of plunging into death and being reborn to life, although perhaps this is no consolation prize.

What we have seen so far allows us to return to our starting point—the island of Crete and the dancing place prepared for Ariadne in Knossos. There, among the ruins of the palace, an inscription in pre-Homeric Greek was found, which spoke of a Lady of the Labyrinth to be offered honey. We know that this, even before ambrosia, was the preferred food of the gods all over the Mediterranean[8] and furthermore, "sweet as honey" were called the gods of the Underworld, whose benevolence was seen as something essential to be procured, through offerings and sacrifices.

Ariadne, who in the legend of the Minotaur was the daughter of Minos, originally seems to have been a sort of goddess of the Realm of the Dead to the Greeks. One could "enter her Realm dancing, just like dancing one could favourably get out of it" (Kerényi, 1983, p. 116; translated for this edition). It is likely that the Lady of the Labyrinth to whom honey was offered at Knossos was Ariadne herself, considered a goddess of the Underworld, and that the Homeric dancing place was a depiction of the realm over which the goddess ruled, as "before Homer, the Underworld was thought as a spiral labyrinth; the *possibility* to come back from that world was begged as pardon from the Queen of the Dead" (Kerényi, 1983, p. 169; translated for this edition). Ariadne "the pure" thus seems to correspond to the figure of Persephone who could free someone from the world of Hades and lead them back to life, and who could return to life herself.

We shall suspend the tale here as the symbol of the *daídalon* has already made numerous images flash before our eyes, although many more could perhaps have materialised from the darkness of millennia, if only we stopped a moment longer to look. The Cretan palace temple, the natural caverns and underground caves with their intricate tunnels, the double-edged axe defined as a ritual implement, the Underworld with its chthonic powers, those who have lived and died, the sacred dances depicting the rebirth that follows walking "into death", to then re-emerge to the light, and the figure of Ariadne as a goddess are all realistically part of the same universe of meaning.

The labyrinth, an unsaturated image which in some respect condenses and refers to this universe of meaning, does not belong, as we have seen, only to the Minoan or to the Greek civilisation, which later took its place in the heart of the Mediterranean; the labyrinth seems to emerge from the depths of the unconscious of the human being, clearly testified by the fact that in its essential form, that of curvilinear meanders, it has been found almost everywhere.

Kerényi, who knew Jung very well, rightly states that in order to understand where this image flows from, we must turn to "another natural spring, a deeper level of the soul, no more confronted to the individual, but to the world itself" (Kerényi, 1983, p. 69; translated for this edition).

From the darkness of this natural spring, at different latitudes and in distant eras, the numinous image of the labyrinth has emerged.

Jung probably would have called it an archetypal image.

## CHAPTER THREE

# Main theme—Possibility

It should come as no surprise that from even this cursory exploration of the archipelago of meaning of the labyrinth such a broad collection of aspects has emerged, interdependent, referring to one another but, at the same time, hinting at further references, revealing and re-veiling, in an apparently infinite chain. All this takes place whenever one comes into contact with a symbol.

From 1921 onwards, C. G. Jung developed a widespread theory of the symbol as an operating reality. This was, in the words of Mario Trevi,[1]

> an independent activity of the psyche, aiming at synthesising conscious and unconscious contents in order to *open up new paths* to the libido, to design unexplored dimensions for the incessant work of the energy, which forms the dynamic basis of man's psychic becoming.
>
> (Trevi, in Jung & Kerényi, 1969, pp. 4–5; translated for this edition, italics added)

Sign and symbol refer to two radically different concepts.

Defined by the phrase *aliquid stat pro aliquo*, a sign is "something that is in place of" what it means to say. Therefore a sign substitutes certain content with another that is related by some connection and that has a conventional meaning (one example is the "no entry" sign, resulting from a convention to which, internationally, we all adhere) or expressed by analogy (the example given by Jung is the winged wheel worn by employees of the railway, a sign indicating that the wearer belongs to the railway company).

The symbol, on the other hand, can be described as *per symbolum aliquid aliud fit*, that is to say, through the symbol content is transformed into something else. It is the best possible formulation, at that time, of complex content, relatively unknown, inexplicable, transcendent, or not fully grasped by the consciousness. A true symbol aims to express the unutterable, referring, alluding, but never signi-fying according to the parameters of the rational consciousness. A symbol remains alive, declares Jung, until it performs the function of implying largely unknown content in the best way possible.

In addition to this property, the symbol also has a metapoetic function, as a transformer, a creator. Unlike what is allowed by the Aristotelian principles of identity, of non-contradiction, and of *tertium non datur* which govern the rational consciousness, the symbol is able to hold opposing, contradictory, and polymorphous psychic contents together, thus feeding an energetic tension, and managing to creatively transcend them.

The transcendent function of the symbol (its ability to resolve the contradiction between opposites, maintaining the life-giving tension, and producing new content without deleting the original) characterises the functioning of the human psyche and speaks volumes for its crea-tive and transformative abilities.

The etymological root of the verb "to interpret", from the Latin *inter pretium*, refers to the meaning of "to mediate", as does the Greek word "hermeneutics", whose root refers to Hermes, the messenger between the two worlds, that of light and that of shadow. According to another explanation, "to interpret" apparently derives from the verb *impetrare*, or "to ask", an action that is altogether different from merely decoding or channelling disguised content into a known system.

Whatever its etymology, interpretation of a symbol (as with a dream), the "asking it to speak", produces only references, allusions, but it can-not exhaust its meaning. In other words, it cannot saturate it. On the periphery of what you seek to clarify, there will always be an indefinite and indefinable aura. If it were fully explained and understood, the symbol as such would die out, become a sign, and retain a primarily historical value. "The quest for meaning", as Galimberti puts it, "beyond meanings established by reason, involves overcoming the limits of reason itself", and this transcendence makes way for a symbolical horizon which "puts together all that reason drives apart" (Galimberti, 1997, pp. 15–16; translated for this edition).

It is Kerényi, once more, who clearly highlights to what extent the labyrinth is a symbol and not a sign. Citing the philosopher and theologian Guardini, he talks respectively of "mystery" and "problem", and writes:

> A problem must be solved, and once solved, it disappears. The mystery, instead, must be experienced, worshipped; it has to join our life. A mystery that can be cleared, solved with an explanation, has never been such. An authentic mystery withstands "explanation" […] because it cannot be explained, in its own nature, or solved rationally.
>
> (Kerényi, 1983, p. 31; translated for this edition)

Like the mystery, therefore, the symbol cannot truly be explained and rationalised. Its meaning eludes us, suggests, does not define, and the same thing happens with all products of the incessant symbolic activity of our psyche such as dreams, fantasies, inner images, creative acts, but also symptoms, lapsus, parapraxes, and so on.

When exploring the universe of meaning which the symbol of the labyrinth opens up, we must content ourselves with capturing references and suggestions, and certainly not seek to explain it once and for all.

For example, defining the labyrinth as a graphic representation of the Underworld would reduce it to a mere sign. Although the reference to the Underworld seems to be an emerging and widespread feature in its interpretation, we must remember that this is not the only one. The references made by a symbol are necessarily manifold and interlinked, "thrown together", as the etymology of the word "symbol" itself indicates (sym-balléin).

The allusion to which we will make most reference in this work is Possibility, as we will see later.

If we embrace the theory of the labyrinth as an archetypal image, we would be consequently led to consider the existence of the archetype from which the image itself originates.

The concept of the archetype and related aspects of the collective unconscious are among the most controversial legacies of the Jungian theory. So as not to run the (ever present) risk of being misunderstood or accused of running with dated and obsolete conceptualisations, we must pause for a second on this aspect and shed some light on the meaning we ascribe to it here. By doing so, we would like to promote a deeper understanding of the theory behind this work, especially for readers less familiar with the complexity of Jungian theory.

To summarise the definition of the symbol given by Volume VI of the *Collected Works* of Jung, we find the statement that:

> The living symbol formulates an essential unconscious factor, and the more widespread this factor is, the more general is the effect of the symbol, for it touches a corresponding chord in every psyche.
>
> (Jung, 1921, p. 477)

This "corresponding chord" is not something that can be easily recognised in conscious life, but rather it belongs to that collection of psychic phenomena which lack the quality of consciousness: the unconscious.

At the start of the last century, the Swiss psychiatrist conducted his research on the word-association test at the Burghölzli psychiatric hospital and showed the extent to which mental processes and content that are not conscious exist and affect the egoic functions. Many experiments conclusively revealed how the ego is unaware of vast areas of psychic activity and how it can, at specific moments, come into contact with some of these.

Jung broadened Freud's initial definition of the unconscious as a mere repository of the repressed. This part of the psyche, defined by Jung as "the personal unconscious", contains lost memories, perceptions, sensations, emotions, events, repressed thoughts, independent content, "feeling-toned complexes", but also all the content that has never been conscious because it does not have sufficient energy to enter into the sphere of consciousness.

Based, once again, on his clinical experience,[2] Jung postulates the existence of a further layer of the unconscious, the so-called "collective unconscious", whose content has never been conscious, nor acquired individually over the course of one's life. This is content that the psyche has in some way inherited in relation to functioning and potentiality— essentially drives, instincts, and archetypes.[3]

Various definitions of the concept of the archetype can be found in many of Jung's works, which has led on occasions to dissent over its ultimate meaning. This fascinating concept, along with the collective unconscious and the "objective psyche", has not been free of timely and sensible criticisms that have highlighted its incomplete, contradictory, and sometimes darkly dogmatic aspects. In this regard, we can consider the critical work of Trevi as a valuable aid in maintaining a de-mythologising attitude towards Jungian metaphors which are less well anchored to the empiricism that always distinguished Jung himself. Suggesting the existence of unknowable, inherited, and invariant metastoric elements in essence could appear to be a regression to naturalistic theories, and a grave contradiction, in terms of a presumed objectification of structures, with regard to the typological relativism of any psychological theory, always subjective.

The archetype seen as an empty shape, a collective predisposition to the formation of images, poses serious problems in terms of investigating mechanisms for its hereditary transmission over the history of mankind. The efforts made by Jung to give it a theoretical basis do not seem to hold up to serious attempts at interrogation. Trevi himself believes archetypes to be an unhappy and unproven metaphor, which "seems to fix the fate of the individual to an a-historical preconditioning, and removes the psyche itself from its undeniable relationship with culture" (Trevi, 1991, p. 96; translated for this edition).

Opposite to this critical stance, there is a position of unconditional adherence, which, first, confuses the concept of the archetype with that of archetypal images, namely the recognisable and culture-specific forms in which an archetype can manifest itself. Blindly believing that in every human being, at whatever latitude and in any age, there are figures such as the Great Mother, the Wise Old Man, the Divine Child, the archetypal Shadow, the Hero, dragons, demons, gods, and so on, like a complete set of "nativity figures" that inhabits the collective unconscious, seems a frankly reductive view, which Jung himself seems, at times, to have embraced and which does not capture the difference between "predisposition to" and cultural and historical "form". The idea of listing an archetypal set in specific forms, its reduction to a packet of contents, and its elevation to explanation of any psychic phenomenon in a dogmatic and definitive manner can also be contested.

So what to think of the notion of archetype? Are there ways to define it that are useful for helping us to understand the activity of the psyche? Somewhere between denial of all theoretical integrity and uncritising glorification, might there be other value for the archetype? Is it really a dated and expendable concept?

In *Psychological Types*, Jung declares that "The peculiar nature of the individual psyche appears less in its elements than in its complex formations" (Jung, 1921, p. 447). If the individual is defined as a collection of elements and his or her uniqueness comes from the specific combination of these, it is probable that in the complex human configuration that has taken shape historically and culturally, certain basic elements may be, so to speak, universal and invariant, as can be seen with materials, where a few essential elements (the atomic particles) can be combined into multiple inorganic and organic structures, giving shape to all material things, depending on an infinite number of physical, chemical, biological, and ultimately historical conditions.

Here the archetype is defined as a *predisposition to perceive and organise experience*, both that which takes place from birth, discovering the outside world, and that which takes place internally, in perception *in primis* of primary needs. The archetype appears to be a concept with operational value, if it is viewed as an emerging quality of the unconscious psyche when it is embodied in the physical reality of the individual and on a cultural level at a certain moment in history.

It seems to be undeniable that members of the human race share a series of potential species-specific ways to relate to the world and with each other.[4] In the field of linguistics, Noam Chomsky expresses a similar concept when he states that the mental structures underlying universal grammar are innate and common to all members of the human race. It is clear that pre-disposed structures, or *a priori* disposed structures, do not act automatically, from within, but rather must be triggered, activated (Jung would say "constellated") by relational experiences.

This can be seen in the oldest study ever conducted in this field, that of Frederick II, the Holy Roman Emperor, who, wondering whether children's language is innate or learned, isolated a group of abandoned children in the fortress of Castel dell'Ovo in Naples for a few months. Nobody spoke a word to them, with the result that none of them developed any form of language.[5]

Studies on attachment, infant and transcultural observation also show a series of archaic characteristics, typical of human beings, of the invariants that we could conclude to be transmissible. The patterns of behaviour that human beings possess through belonging to the human species and not through learning, as is the case with all species of animal, allow us to speculate over certain characteristics that are in some way coded and transmitted from one generation to another.

A definition of archetype, among the many proposed by Jung, which goes along the same lines as the ones we are exploring could be: "The archetype would be a structural quality or condition peculiar to a psyche that is somehow connected with the brain" (Jung, 1938/1940, p. 104).[6] In the concept of the archetype (suggested by Jung himself as a temporary definition, subject to change, when it proves no longer effective for making the set of phenomena it was designed to capture intelligible), we similarly find the expression of a reality that is experientially detectable in its effects.

Perhaps, to avoid misunderstandings, the term should be changed, a new word invented. If I had to hazard one, I would use the word "pre-disposal". In all honesty, this name is much less evocative than the original, but the fact remains that it tries to describe that "something that wasn't learned" either from direct personal experience or from the culture which shapes us as a species.

It seems difficult to contest the fact that human beings are united by a set of dispositions to perceive, elaborate, and process (often through images, but not always) the internal and external realities. How this species-specific heritage passes down is mysterious, as it is the missing link between genetic code, protein synthesis, formation of structures and behaviours.

The metastoric aspect of the archetype is such from the perspective of the consciousness, which is the only perspective that we can adopt. Moreover, the ego that sometimes comes across an inner image (in a dream, a fantasy, an intuition, or while playing) which represents a motive or a function that has not been learned from direct personal experience nor from the immense store of experience of others represented by culture (collective conscious), rightly feels it is in the presence of something that transcends it, which comes from "beyond".

If the personal unconscious is principally a place for repressed content, which has been conscious or which is "born" of an encounter with reality (feeling-toned complexes), for those elements which come from this "elsewhere", it is legitimate to assume a "further unconscious", as Trevi would call it. Where we find specifically human subjects, motives, and functions, such as those represented in different times and places in stories, rites, religions, myths, fantasies, delusions, visions, dreams, games, and so on, one can risk using the term "collective".

Returning then to the image of the labyrinth, in particular the classical labyrinth, which, as we have seen, is present in many different cultures and historical eras, it could well belong to that set of images which may come from this "further unconscious". One characteristic that these images often show is a numinous quality—Freud might also add "uncanny". Finding oneself in the presence of a labyrinth, even just an effigy, evokes a certain mood, a mixture of fascination and fear, just as places full of history or the wildest scenes in nature can evoke.

One might, advisedly, be struck by an aspect of the definition of the labyrinth that is often found in dictionaries of symbols. Such a definition would contain the complication of its layout and the difficulty of the journey as essential elements.

Now, although these may be two elements that belong to the labyrinth in their various forms, we do not believe that they represent its distinctive trait.

To understand what this is, we noticed that Kerényi posed a rhetorical question illuminating but neglecting, in our opinion, the implications and intimate pregnancy of meaning: he wonders whether the essential characteristic is not "the fact that *the labyrinth has always a way out*, despite its tortuosities?" (Kerényi, 1983, p. 32; translated for this edition). The peculiar characteristic of a labyrinth is that, despite its complications and the tortuosity of the path, there is always the *way in which is also the way out*. If we imagine ourselves physically in a labyrinth, in one of its numerous meanders, knowing that somewhere there is a way out could be our motivation to search for salvation, which otherwise we would almost certainly give up on. Knowing that there is a way out, or even just the hope that one exists, is, in the most varied experiences of human beings and even animals (in this regard, see Chapter Four), a *conditio sine qua non* of action.

Making reference to historical periods that precede even the Greek myth of Theseus by centuries, our hypothesis is that, with the symbol of the labyrinth, an image emerges from the unconscious which depicts *Possibility* or at least the *hope of Possibility*.

From what we are told in the famous myth, the stratagem of the thread of Ariadne, tied to that one entrance, represented the only hope of salvation, the only way to return to the light. Within the *daídalon*, a way out exists, and it is possible to find it or find it again, even if the journey is difficult and fraught with risk—the risk of wandering lost along its identical passages until eternity, of meeting the Minotaur, the monster, "the Other", or "the Other within ourselves", the unconscious, a meeting that can enrich in the sense of individuation, but that can also destroy and annihilate.

We can try to return to the light transformed, but we may perish in the process of doing so. Possibility, in summary, does not mean "certainty" at all (in this regard, see Chapter Eight).

Why might we see the labyrinth as an image of Possibility?

To take some of the references made previously, the Underworld, to which the labyrinth often seems to be linked, is defined as a world with which *it is possible* to have dialogue. Certainly, not all men are permitted to enter into the kingdom of Hades, but many myths tell how this was possible for certain exceptional people. *Deo concedente* (indeed, considering that the historical-mythological search depicts female chthonian deities, perhaps in this case it would be more correct to say *Dea concedente*) *can* enter into the Realm of the Dead and return to life renewed.

Ariadne, in Crete, and Persephone are mythical testimonies of the idea of the *possibility* of returning to the light, after descending into the Underworld.

The crossroad in classical labyrinths in northern Europe, those with two paths (as the *labrys* was also double, the double-edged axe), refers to *possibility*: salvation, the virgin in the centre, renewed life from contact with the god of the Underworld, on one hand; death, no return, and entrapment in the dead end, on the other.

Theseus, who dances like the crane, celebrating with his friends the success of his mission to kill the Minotaur and thus free the city of Athens from the heavy tribute of blood ordered by Minos for killing his son, performs a dance of joy for *realised possibility*. It was not a mission for which success was certain, even for the Athenian hero, as the fact that he took with him white veils and black veils, to be hoisted on the masts upon return to indicate success or failure, respectively, testifies.

Each of the ritual dances described previously and which reproduce the image of the classical labyrinth, such as the *Maro* Indonesian rite dance, the dance represented on the shield of Achilles, Greek-inspired dances staged by the Romans, in which dancers held in their hands a rope and the already explored Scandinavian *Jungfrudans*, seem to be connected to the representation of entry and return, entry into the mysterious immobile silence of Death and return to Life, re-discovered, renewed. All these dances seem to represent a ritual omen of *being able* to re-emerge into the light.

In confrontation with the unconscious, the ego finds it is the subject, in the dual meaning of "active protagonist", on the one hand, and of *sub-jectum*, "subject to", uncontrollable forces, by the other. Just as the ego is exposed to the possibility of greater individuation or to the disturbing fear of inflation, being in the labyrinth, despite the difficulties, despite the tortuosity of the distressing journey, despite the sense of being lost, we know that *we may* indeed perish but that *we may* also escape—that a way out exists and *can* be found.

Even if we have lost ourselves, we are not necessarily lost.

Defined in this way, the universe of meaning to which the symbol of the labyrinth refers seems to have a common denominator in Possibility.

Taking a symbolic image or mythical tale as a paradigm for understanding and illustrating psychic content, a clinical concept, or a psychological mechanism, always involves some risk: that of stressing the phenomena that can be seen in the image or the myth itself. The labyrinth possesses such a powerful force of attraction that we could become trapped in its passages if we do not take sufficient care. For example, physically, the image of the labyrinth brings to mind the existence of one way out, one and one alone, of a sole possibility, when it is clear that situations in life often have more than one.

The concept of Possibility, expressed through the image of the labyrinth, should be taken as an absolute value, so to speak, by extracting the concept, removing it from the physical image. Only then can it be productively used as a key to understanding psychic activity, and this is what we will try to illustrate over the course of this work.

Jung maintained that an archetype, when it is constellated, could manifest itself in images—for example, figures or personalities in dreams, in the active imagination, or psychotic symptoms.

At a specific point in his vast body of work, he speaks instead of a group of archetypes which are not necessarily personified. These archetypes would represent a *process* as such, and he defines them as "archetypes of transformation": "They are not personalities, but are typical situations, places, ways and means, that symbolize the kind of transformation in question" (Jung, 1934/1954, p. 38). The mandala, symbols of quaternity, and the symbol of the entwined couple are, according to Jung, examples of images originating from constellated archetypes of transformation. In light of the references to the possibility of perishing or escaping, to the death–rebirth process, to renewal, it is likely that the labyrinth is an image originating from a "pre-disposal" of this kind, which could justifiably be called "an archetype of Possibility".

Being related to a process, it will not necessarily lead to dream images of labyrinths, although this may happen.[7] Much more commonly, the archetype of Possibility may manifest itself in dreams, images, fantasies, or while playing in an ever-changing multitude of situations in which the topic of "possibility" can be seen and linked to the specific journey of the patient in therapy.

Contact with unconscious aspects that belong to them, accompanied by intense affects, can make the patient (and also the therapist) feel a shared sense of opening up meaning, or the possibility of a new direction. Furthermore, we do not think that it is necessary to postulate an opposite archetype as well (as in the case, for example, of the paternal archetype, positive or negative), as the word "possible" suggests both a positive and negative outcome simultaneously (in this regard, see Chapter Eight).

Thus, in conclusion, far from treating the concept of the labyrinth as a trivial metaphor of the tortuous journey of working with a patient, what we are suggesting here is that it is an image originating from an archetype of transformation, the constellation of which could be of vital importance in the course of the therapy process.

Other theories of the psyche have revealed and described the same topic with different images and words, but the operating mechanism seems to be the same.

# PART II

## CHORUS

## CHAPTER FOUR

# Main verses—Possibility, right to existence, and ego complex

L et us take up the narrative again from the series of reflections that led us to Possibility, the initial chords that were struck in the main theme: observing what happened with patients following a supervision session or personal reflection between one session and another, and having highlighted the widespread use of spatial metaphors to describe the mental process within a therapeutic relationship. This brought us to the image of the labyrinth, and finally to the hypothesis of an archetype of Possibility.

At the same time as these themes were developing, another image sprung to mind, or rather a memory: it was regarding research carried out by Martin Seligman, a cognitivist, which I had read about many years earlier, probably in some university text or other. When watching a live research project conducted by Solomon on Pavlovian conditioning in 1964, Seligman became interested in a curious phenomenon that had apparently undermined this research—the dogs used in the experiments were no longer cooperating and were not behaving in the way expected. Over the course of the following year, Seligman prepared his research on what he came to define as "learned helplessness".

Here is a brief description of it: in the first part of the research, a group of dogs was made to enter, one by one, a closed box with an electrified floor. Every dog was subjected to a light but irritating shock, which the dog could stop by pressing a panel with its nose, as the dogs discovered very quickly. A second group of dogs, also subjected to the shock, was unable to stop it, no matter what they did. Finally, a third group of dogs was not subjected to any shocks. With this preparatory stage complete, the dogs were then placed, one by one, into a box with two compartments, divided by a low barrier. In this case, to avoid the shock, all they needed to do was jump over the barrier and reach the other compartment. As Seligman expected, the first and third groups of dogs jumped the barrier in just a few seconds, escaping the shock, whilst the dogs in the second group, who had previously learned that their actions were ineffective, sat ruefully, suffering the shock.

This dual-compartment box is comparable to a representation of a very simplified labyrinth, in which the way out is rather obvious. Without going into much detail on studies of learned helplessness here, let us highlight one point that is very striking: how can a dog learn behaviour that in some way goes against their instinct for survival and avoiding pain? Cognitivists show that the latter instinct is conditionable but do not investigate the origins of the instinct itself. Where does it come from?

From what we can understand, the instinct comes from the unconscious mind, and it is improbable that a mere effort of the consciousness would be sufficient to condition it (in dogs, we can speculate that the consciousness shines less brightly than in human beings). In fact, in this experimental situation, the dog learns about *not being able*. We can say that the dog "knows" there is no escape route, knowledge that acts as an obstacle to any further action, in surprising contrast with the instinct which would motivate it to look for one. Thus, it seems plausible to speculate that dogs too, in a way that is difficult for us to represent, have an archetypal aspect pre-disposing to Possibility, and this is in some way inhibited in the aforementioned experiments, as only another unconscious factor could block out powerful unconscious content such as an instinct.[1]

We can speculate that instincts and archetypes are found in that area of the psyche that is grounded in biology and that human beings should not differ very much from animals in this respect, but rather in terms of development of a more complex consciousness. Based on this, it is possible to draw a parallel between the behaviour of the dogs in the experiments described above and that of a patient undergoing a course of therapy.

We are not declaring that just as the dog can come to "not know" that it is possible to avoid the shock, the patient does not know that he can "heal", and that therefore the central factor in a therapy process is simply suggesting to the patient that *there is a way out, you can do it.* Rather, we aim to reflect on the role that *perception of an unconscious possibility* can have in therapy or, to express the same concept in Jungian terms, the constellation of the archetype of transformation, which we have dubbed *daídalon.*[2]

Jung himself does away with the idea that simply suggesting to the patient that "they can heal" is therapeutic in itself, where he states that:

> [...] a suggestion is never accepted without an inner readiness for it, or if after great insistence it is accepted, it is immediately lost again. A suggestion that is accepted for any length of time always presupposes a marked psychological readiness which is merely brought into play by the so-called suggestion.

> (Jung, 1916/1957, p. 75)

Even if at times the hope of seeing the patient "improved", "healed", "grown", in better balance with their own unconscious, can lead the therapist to be more or less explicitly encouraging, to say between the lines "chin up, you can do it", all of this rarely translates into effective growth, healing, or better balance. Suggestion is not enough if there is not "a marked psychological readiness". Whatever could Jung be referring to?

In search of an answer to this question, it is useful to add a statement made by Frey-Rohn, where she maintains that:

> a balance of opposites would depend on a gradient and could never be the result of a merely voluntary effort. Transformations and changes of ideas, therefore, called for the natural happening of differences in potential, provided they tended in the correct *direction.*

> (Frey-Rohn, 1974, p. 171, italics added)

In the energetic point of view, to which the author makes reference here, Jung states that psychic energy, which along with Freud he initially called *libido*, requires a difference of potential between two contents of opposite kinds to unfold.

As is the case with physics, the difference of potential generates a gradient which allows energy to flow in a sense and to make itself available. In this respect, in the imaginal language that often characterises his work, Jung writes: "It has become abundantly clear to me that life can flow forward only along *the path* of the gradient" (Jung, 1917/1926/1943, p. 53). In essence, there must be a gradient, produced by the difference of potential between two opposites, to ensure that psychic energy does not stagnate, or simply regress, but to enable it to continue its flow. The word "gradient", to stick with the world of spatial metaphors and the image of the labyrinth, could also be substituted by the words "way", "path", leaving the meaning of the phrase intact.

Using the energetic metaphor, when there is a gradient in the unconscious, the patient's consciousness can come to learn of its existence in the relationship with the analyst who knows how to read its signs and effects: feeling-tones, memories, body sensations, images, fantasies, and symbols. Perhaps the "marked psychological readiness" that Jung referred to is the activation of content that expresses the possibility of a "way out".

A point of fundamental interest in clinical practice is identifying what promotes healing. I cannot be satisfied by the statement that, over a course of psychotherapy, the "therapeutic factor" is generally "the personality of the analyst", above and beyond their theoretical background, as is periodically suggested by research on the effectiveness of various methods, and by Jung himself.[3]

In its conception, analytical treatment is a dialectical process (nowadays, we would perhaps say "dialogic") in which the analyst is involved as much as the patient.[4] The personality of the analyst is, in the language used by analytical psychology, the combination of the conscious and unconscious of the analyst him- or herself and their mutual relationship, which produces what Jung happily described as the "personal equation".

Patients who have a relationship with a therapist are, in turn, a conscious–unconscious system which relates to the conscious–unconscious system of the analyst, with its own characteristics. This relational crossroads, according to Jung, finds its roots in a layer common to both parties, the collective unconscious.

In an image, we can think of the collective layer of the unconscious as if it were the common ground precisely where the roots (the personal unconscious) of two flowers, which are the two subjects of the relationship, are found. Another significant aspect of the relational crossroads is formed by the cultural references of the collective consciousness in which the two subjects are immersed. To stay with the image, this could be represented by the air surrounding the two flowers which both, so to speak, "breathe", in an exchange process between internal and external.

It is known that the personal equation, like any equation, has variables (so called when we know the nature of them) and unknowns (when, on the other hand, we do not know the nature of them). One of the variables or, in other words, one of the pieces of unconscious content that belongs to the complexity of the patient's personality could be the archetype of Possibility, constellated in the relationship with the analyst. What might represent the therapeutic factor is that the unconscious of the analyst feels and grasps "the labyrinth in which the patient finds themselves and their way out", the "inner landscape" of the patient and its outlook, the gradient of certain psychic aspects.[5] When this "unconscious knowledge" meets the consciousness of the analyst, it can somehow be reflected/mirrored to the consciousness of the patient, who feels it to be "true" as it comes from deep within him- or herself.

Given that this deals with unconscious content, the consciousness of the patient does not necessarily have a rational understanding of it (as the meaning of a symbol cannot be grasped rationally), but experiences principally its feeling-tone, perceiving it to be authentic content, his or her own, because it moves something in him or her (compare the etymology of "e-motion", from Latin *ex-movere*), it strikes a chord.

For Jung, affect is the crucial element in psychic energy, and it is particularly through consciously welcoming feeling-toned content that the ego dialogues with the unconscious. Thus, it is not saying "you can do it" that heals, but, if it should correspond to the patient's unconscious content, simply saying "you can do it" could, potentially, trigger significant change.

* * *

Rebecca, a young woman, arrived at my room with clear symptoms of depression. The dreams she came with in the early stages of analysis kept her awake, feeling very anxious.

The common denominator of the different situations played out in her dream theatre was her being put down by various figures, sometimes work colleagues, sometimes members of her family, and other significant figures, such as ex-fiancés. She herself, in the dream, felt a distressing sense of self-deprecation, due to not listening to and not meeting her own needs.

While, on the one hand, I was very concerned about the suffering felt by the patient, with whom I empathised, on the other, I pointed out that dreams of this kind seemed, for the most part, to highlight a very central theme to her, a sort of extreme severity towards herself with which it seemed to be very important to get into contact. I reckoned she continued to dream about this aspect so that we could take it into account and examine its basic elements.[6]

The patient was perfectly aware of this severity towards herself. She did not like herself physically and thought she was fat and ugly (although she was actually a good-looking woman); she had never had a good relationship with her body and did have quite a bad sex life. Lately she had been sleeping little, crying often for no apparent reason, and feeling great aggression which was released, mostly verbally, against her family, leaving her feeling even more despicable and out of sorts.

Rebecca had in her history a sad story of being abused by her father, an event that took place during middle school, preceded by years of cumulative trauma from a home environment in which, due to parental work commitments, little time was devoted to her needs, leaving her feeling a deep sense of abandonment. She believed that her problems had been caused by the abuse, whilst I felt that the "seeds" of her discomfort had somehow been sown much earlier.

As with the dreams that Rebecca zealously brought to me, surprisingly, I could see a sense of possibility that she herself was consciously not aware of at all. My reflections were therefore coming up against the more obvious sense of pain from the dream scenarios and did not seem to open up new perspectives in any way. Actually, as if to prove me wrong, in one session Rebecca brought a clear worsening of symptoms. She had eaten practically nothing all week, and when, with great effort, she had tried to eat, overwhelming nausea had made her vomit almost immediately. It was the first time that anything of this nature had happened, as she had never before had problems related to food.

By treating this physical symptom as if it were a dream, interesting associations were brought to light, significantly linked to the fact that she would have liked to have been thinner than she was, as thin as when she was a teenager. These associations allowed me to tell her that what seemed to common sense like a worsening of symptoms (the nausea and vomiting) was perhaps a valuable example of an attempt to cure herself.

The patient was very surprised by this interpretation, but it seemed possible to me that her not eating was an attempt to be thinner and to like herself better, in a period when not liking herself was the main topic of our sessions. Furthermore, the nausea clearly represented the physiological reaction to wanting to expel something which the body feels is harmful, and I thus made the connection with the content loaded with anger which, usually, the patient repressed until she exploded.

In other words, one could speculate that a part of her was somehow looking out for herself and that certain things could no longer be "pushed down".

Observing that part of her was taking care of her (although not really in a very useful way, like not eating or vomiting) allowed me to implicitly reflect a very strong sense of possibility to her. There was not only the severe and derogatory side within her but also another side, which was trying to take care of her.

In the following session, the patient mentioned that the nausea was gone and she was once again eating normally, as if it were nothing. Still, rather than linger on this point, she continued to be surprised by what I had told her. But I was even more surprised at her when she recounted this dream:

> I am in a group of people on a journey through the mountains. We are hungry and thirsty but we have run out of supplies. There is a guy in group who is urging us to move on. We arrive at a small lake but on the bottom and all around it, there are dead people everywhere. The water is poisoned. We can only keep going. The city is still far off and without water we will not make it. We arrive at a sort of castle, a little fort, which seems to be deserted. We look around for any sign of someone but there are not many alive. Once again, we find so many dead people. A snowstorm begins and we decide to stop. Luckily, there are bottles of water, not many, but they will help us to survive for a bit. Time goes by, and we are so scared of dying. We know that sixty-one water pipes have been poisoned, we have to warn the city but the phone won't connect. We need to go higher. I find myself suspended in the air with two

balloons. There is a signal, we can make a call. It connects, and I phone my best friend first to tell her, thinking that I am going to die, that I have reflected on so many things, that my life has been wrong and that I want to live it differently.

The scene depicted in the dream is a tortuous journey in search of salvation, in an atmosphere of great danger of death. Primary needs, such as hunger and thirst, cannot be satisfied as the water has been poisoned and the city is far away and at risk of being contaminated by the poison.

There is the guy who pushes everyone to move forward, an unknown positive male figure, whom Rebecca says is her contemporary (it could be, in Jungian terms, a positive animus figure, which has been activated during the course of therapy or a representation of me, as I was actually the patient's contemporary), and at a certain point in the dream, unexpected resources appear, the bottles of water, which allow them to go on a bit further and to satisfy a vital need.

Finally, the dream shows the possibility of communication (the phone) and eventually being rescued. I remember that when I recounted this dream to my supervisor, he underlined the magical quality of the solution chosen by the unconscious. The patient flying from two balloons, to look for a signal, is not a very likely scenario. Although this interpretation warned me not to fall prey to easy enthusiasms, I interpreted this dream as a necessary first step, a signal of a change of perspective. The dream depicts a journey towards the possibility of salvation. Today, I would define this event as a signal of constellation, within the therapeutic relationship, of the archetype of the *daídalon*.

The motivating effect of having captured a prospective meaning in the worsening symptoms of the previous session also extended to the following session, in which Rebecca told me about another particularly significant dream:

> I am in my parents' house and the whole family is there. I am feeling anxious. Somebody wants to hurt me and has started to strike down the people I love. They are buried alive.
>
> I hear cries coming from the garden, I go out to see what is happening and my brother tells me that it is better that I don't see. They have found another body.

I manage to get close, I recognise him. It's a boy I was with years ago. I start to cry and suddenly he opens his eyes: he's alive! I start to think that the person who wishes me harm and who is behind all this is my father.

I go back into the house and get a feeling of imminent danger.

Someone is hidden, lying in wait to kill me. Suddenly a shadow throws itself at me and I realise that it is a little girl. It is ME as a little girl.

When I recall Rebecca's dream, I am still greatly moved and get goose-bumps. In the scenario of the family home, the setting of the abuse no less, a strong sense of anxiety awakens and content from her past is buried alive, with her great suffering.

Repressing the past causes pain because it is a past that lives on. But the frightening figure turns out to be herself as a child, a confirmation of the fact that, even before the abuse by her father, there was the whole history of childhood neglect to provoke a huge sense of self-destructive rage.

Getting in contact with this scary childhood self is a fundamental step, the dream seemed to say. You must embrace the aggression and somehow disempower it. Rebecca, too, saw this dream as something very valuable, immediately after the previous dream which had shown her the possibility of salvation.

In sequence, the two dreams seem to show a viable path, and both the patient and I considered it a turning point in her therapeutic journey, which was still long and agonising, due to external events which allowed her to give up on the steps she had taken, and to surrender herself to the persecutory aspects within (the same ones that had driven her to attempt suicide in her early adolescence).

Without going into the merits of the case, of which I have deliberately given little history, I have presented this precious material with the intention of highlighting with a clinical example the importance of constellation of the archetype of Possibility.

In that stage of therapy, I tried to actively position myself so that the patient would be aware of it, feeling (initially, probably unconsciously, and then later more knowingly) that *it was possible* to do it and, little by little, as analysis went on, feeling the motivational effect first hand.

Rebecca, who had always been treated as an "object", to move from one place to another, to leave at her grandparents' house to suit the family's work commitments, her need to be "seen" and valued in life ignored, used and abused, not only sexually, by her father, but also psychologically by partners who she met later in life, slowly emerged as a "subject". A subject able to give profound value to what was within and, more and more, to stand up to both people around her who continued to treat her as an "object" and that inner persecutory part which colluded with her abusers.

I believe that the possibility of passing from "object" to "subject" was initially shown to the patient by her dreams, and only when this was captured and reflected was an evolutionary energy activated, slowly and alternately.

* * *

It is now essential to link what we are declaring to what happens in the course of the development of the consciousness. How is what is defined in Jungian terms as the "ego complex" formed?

Jung, consistent with the theoretical attitude of the early days of psychoanalysis, did not devote much time to observation of the early stages of children's lives, but it is possible to draw certain useful notations from his work, sometimes expressed between the lines.

In addition, we can refer to the great clinical and theoretical work carried out by more recent authors, both from the Jungian school (*in primis* Fordham and the so-called English school), and the post- and neo-Freudian school.

Jung considers that a child is very close to being solely unconscious. The ego seems to emerge, like a set of islets, from the great "ocean of unconsciousness" gradually as the newborn relates to important figures in the outside world and with what these experiences constellate or activate in the inner imaginal world. Through endo- and exo-sensorial experiences, the body is the base, the "first island" of the ego complex which, as the name itself suggests, is a complex set of functions, memory, perceptions, and affects. The ego, in the "inner landscape" of the individual, is, amongst other complexes, the one which, despite being in good measure unconscious, has the faculty of consciousness.

A clear and concise description of how the ego emerges from the unconscious can be found in the words of Verena Kast:

> [...] at first, the child is uncoscious of the ego complex, which gradually becomes more conscious through the experience of the physical ego—also known as the physical self—particularly when the child's reactions are perceived, accepted and responded by those who are close to it. In its physicality, which is the basis of the ego-complex, the child attains a sense of acceptance and the *right to existence*.

> (Kast, 1992, p. 57)[7]

If we understand correctly what Kast states, from the experience of self as a body, from the sensations, perceptions, and emotions on their somatic side, the child begins to construct the set of elements and contents which will form the ego complex. All this cannot happen by itself, but can only take place in the presence of a significant subject who gives the child attention, acceptance, and adequately meets their needs.

Therefore, the child, still unconscious, *feels that he or she can exist*, and on this *feeling of having the right to exist*, an "ego" begins to form. "Having the right to exist" is another way to express the topic of possibility with which we are dealing. The child with no name, no identity, feels both being attributed to him by the people taking care of him and *discovers being, after feeling that he can be and before knowing who he is*.

Donald Winnicott seems to express an idea similar to what we are trying to present when he writes, on his concept of "transitional space", that in order for this creative capacity to come to exist, the child must have confidence in the reliability and dependability of the caregiver.[8] The latter and the right to existence that the child "feels" (and when we say "feel", we refer to affects) seem to belong to the same archipelago of meaning, with the difference that whilst the feeling of trust, according to Winnicott, is introjected, in Jungian terms we can say that it constellates a feeling of possibility which already exists in the unconscious, a "potential ego", a pre-disposition to develop a consciousness.

The subjectivity of the child begins to emerge in the relationship with the subjectivity by which he or she feels authorised to exist because he or she is loved. The paradox is that the child already exists but does not know it. It is not the caregiver who gives him or her something that he or she does not have. However, the child, unconsciously, needs a subject to allow him or her to feel that he or she has the right to exist.

According to Winnicott, what happens in the structural phases of the transitional space between significant adult and child is comparable to what should happen in the course of therapy between analyst and patient:

> The behaviour of the analyst [...] by being good enough in the matter of adaptation to need, is gradually perceived by the patient as something that raises a hope that the true self may at last be able to take the risk involved in its starting to experience living. [...] *Good enough adaptation by the analyst* produces a result which is exactly that which is sought, namely, a shift in the patient of the main site of operation from a false to a true self. There is now for the first time in the patient's life an opportunity for the development of an ego.
>
> (Winnicott, 1958, pp. 297–298)

If we define the term "opportunity" as "perception of a possibility" for the ego to develop and to abandon the strenuous defence of the Winnicottian true self, we find a point of convergence with what we are discussing.

It is plausible that the process that leads to the development of the ego complex and the therapeutic process have something in common with the activation of *a sense of possibility within a significant relationship*. This sense of possibility can only be perceived as authentic (by the child and by the patient) if the need or the feeling that the unconscious of the parent or the analyst captures, accepts, and mirrors back, is authentic.

In very similar terms to these, Maddalena Pessina, using the archetypal image of the entwined couple, analyses the issue of what happens in psychotherapy in a work that deals with the transcendent function and the symbol. The words she uses are all related to *perception of a possibility*.[9] The possibility is perceived, first, on an unconscious level by the therapist (in virtue of the "psychic infection" between the patient's unconscious and that of the therapist), but, take note, it is a *possibility that belongs to the patient*. If this is somehow reflected/ mirrored back (made digestible), the archetype of Possibility can constellate, and this could play an essential part in promoting transformations. The archetype will manifest itself in images, whether in dreams or not, and in strong feelings that touch, move, and affect both patient and analyst.

Pessina highlights that the analyst, operating as the transcendent function, carries out a symbolic operation in place of/in the presence of the patient and eventually must rename the symbol

> without words, practically. But in the "same" words as the patient [...] what modifies the affect in the patient is the "knowledge" of the analyst [...], only if the latter can use the same words as the subject, because only these words (and nobody else's) can penetrate to the depths of their unconscious [...] words, but also images.
>
> (Pessina, 2004, pp. 48–49; translated for this edition)

If the possibility really belongs to the patient, then the therapist who captures it and reflects it using the associated words, images, and the affects, brings to the consciousness the constellated archetype of Possibility behind these very images and affects.

In the course of therapy, one often finds oneself in situations where a symptom, discomfort, a dream, some internal images, fantasies, and feelings offer an opportunity for dialogue between the patient's consciousness and emerging unconscious parts, full of potential.

To illustrate the hypothesis described, we could find other examples, but it seems increasingly appropriate to try to think about what happens in the clinical practice of other therapists (not only Jungians) in light of this model. Exploring texts that narrate what happens in clinical practice, from the points of view of the most disparate schools of thought, could provide further material for a fruitful comparison.

## CHAPTER FIVE

# Chorus—possible comparisons

When a text presents clinical cases drawn from the first-hand experience of the author, there is an opportunity to get closer and observe what happens in the closed-off *tèmenos*, the sacred enclosure of the analysis room.

Usually, in the lively narration of his or her own words, the therapist describes certain clinical situations that highlight the points that are in their view crucial, the junctions along the way of the therapeutic journey which mark a turning point in the analytical progress of a given patient.

Susanna Chiesa, for example, illustrates her own experience with patients for whom the body expresses mental discomfort through an eating disorder.[1] When it is the body conveying "other" messages through symptoms, it must not be silenced, by tackling the symptoms according to a medical model to restore functionality, but rather the body must be listened to, in terms of what it is trying to say, avoiding getting bogged down in its concrete dimensions.

When presenting the case of a seventeen-year-old anorexic girl, the author describes the extreme feelings of control and destruction that the patient shows in the session, and her own countertransference, fluctuating between aggression and a sense of guilt. In the third year of analysis, as the patient was describing her own destructive fantasies about food, along with convulsive movements of the hands, the analyst, intuitively tuned in to the body, "saw" in those hands and frenetic finger movements those of newborn children.

> The intensity of the countertransferal fantasy made me ask myself whether her tearing and picking wasn't a wish to be born, and this is what I reflected to her, allowing her to make a shift towards behaviour which had always led to a short circuit between anger and guilt.
>
> (Chiesa, in Wuehl, 2002, p. 108; translated for this edition)

This shift, referred to by the therapist as a turning point, seems to adequately illustrate what we have described previously: perception of a sense of possibility (in this case revealed not in a dream, but by observing body language), reflected to the patient, seems to be able to break down the dominance of the defences which keep pain at bay, cancelling out the symbolic space, thus opening a new path. Although fragile and full of sudden twists and turns, it is, however, possible to proceed.

Later in the text, the author states that what the analyst attempts to do during therapy is to activate the transcendent function, "as a *possibility* of putting into contact the consciousness and the unconscious, inciting the *potential* for change and development" (Chiesa, in Wuehl, 2002, p. 111; translated for this edition). This statement offers us the opportunity to reflect on the adjective "transcendent" which suggests "going beyond", an image that refers once more to spatial metaphor. In the transcendent function, Jung indicates the central pillar of the function of the symbol. The latter is able to transcend the tension between two opposites and the conflict, allowing us to ask ourselves whether the constellation of a sense of possibility might not describe, in different words, a similar psychic phenomenon.

When the patient succeeded in experiencing unconscious potential, unexpected by her conscious ego, her voice expressed the joy and curiosity of one who has discovered a new world, and managed to say "today, now that there is a gap, a difference between what I think and what you reflect back to me, is like a gust of fresh air, a door opening" (Chiesa, in Wuehl, 2002, p. 113; translated for this edition).

Elisabetta Franciosi describes the case of a woman for whom the body also takes centre stage, with a parade of somatic symptoms. These symptoms evoke in the analyst, at times, countertransferential feelings of annoyance and boredom, but also a strong sense of powerlessness. The body, the sole place of feeling, leads the analyst to "try to approach the meaning behind these symptoms with the need to express feelings of anger and of love" and to bear "a feeling which is impossible for the patient" until "discovering, where possible, traces of meaning behind pain which *can* now be expressed" (Franciosi, in Wuehl, 2002, pp. 120–121; translated for this edition).

It is only at this point that the body can cease to be the sole messenger of emotions that cannot be mentally processed, and, as in the case presented above, the perception of meaning (*senso*, therefore direction) behind the wall of bodily symptoms that prevent any possibility of approaching the painful mental areas, reflected to the patient in the context of a relationship so significant as to be invaded by archaic feelings of transference, allows us to constellate the *daídalon*.

The dream following the session in which all this took place is described by the analyst as a pivotal point for change. In the dream, a woman offers the patient food and they both eat for as long as they need to. Franciosi interprets the image of the woman who brings the food as a personification of the analysis, which allows the patient's needs to be addressed. The patient, following this interpretation, commented that in life *you can* also choose what to eat. Being able to choose refers in itself to the dimension of possibility and also, in this case, the event described is considered a turning point (again, a spatial metaphor) in therapy.

When, as with patients of this kind, the analyst finds him- or herself immersed in tales with no emotion, it becomes necessary to tune into "the defensive feeling as only the body, narrated and experienced in the session, leads to a sort of *possibility of meaning*", says Franciosi, and to reflect "what reverberates in the body from the soul, far distant from what I have in front of me. Like a child who feels but does not know what his feeling means" (Franciosi, in Wuehl, 2002, p. 127; translated for this edition).

First, there is the hunger, then the ego.

The libido, the psychic energy, flows out into the world in search of relationships and returns to the subject transformed by the subjects it encounters on its way, both when those subjects respond in a satisfactory manner and when they fail in their task.

Just as happens in the development of the ego complex, the patient is comparable to a child who feels (perceptions, affects, emotions) but does not know either him- or herself or his or her own feelings and requires relationships to recognise him- or herself and to authorise him- or herself to exist, beyond defensive rigidity. When this is felt to be possible, a process of overcoming the symptomatic *impasse* and resumption, in individuative terms, of the relationship between consciousness and unconscious begins.

It is often the case that this sense of possibility can only be conveyed through a painful and engaged confrontation of the strong feelings of angst which the patient brings to sessions. In these cases, one might try to "hold", to support the patient, preventing them collapsing in silent despair, and simultaneously being somewhat encouraging. This is a tension between opposites that is excruciating both for the patient, who experiences the pain first hand, and for the therapist.[2]

During my first personal analysis, an engaging and shattering experience was getting in touch with the oneiric dimension, acknowledging that what came from the nocturnal world was as real and crucial as what belonged to the world of the waking. My dreams, a voice sounding in the darkness, revealed a complex dimension of existence which my consciousness did not even suspect.

The value of the dream in the economy of the psyche seemed to me to be even more important in relationships with the patients who have come to my analysis room. Each time a dream is recounted to me, I approach it with the reverence accorded to sacred objects and allow its interpretation to be coloured by what the dream evokes in me as a countertransferential reaction, not only in terms of reflections and interpretations, but also, and in particular, through my images and experiences, like inner chords sounding as if in sympathy.

One of the functions of the dream which best fits with the hypothesis suggested in this work is highlighted by Jung when he says that "[...] it often happens that other *possibilities for developing* the personality lie buried somewhere or other in the past, unknown to anybody, not even to the patient" (Jung, 1931, p. 43, italics added).

In my experience, first as a patient and then as a therapist, the discovery of other possibilities for development often comes about by listening to what emerges from the depths of the unconscious psyche.

The word "enigma" (from the Greek *àinigma*) means "the darkness speaks", and it is implied that what emerges from the darkness cannot have the characteristics of clarity, of explanation. The voice of darkness evokes, shows, alludes to, and indicates, remaining somewhat mysterious, as we have previously seen to be the case with the symbol. In the same work, Jung defines "prophetic dreams", that reconnoitre, those specific dreams which contain "inklings of possibilities".

I think that Rebecca's first dream, described above, can be considered to be of this nature. In the dream, we can see the creative forces of the unconscious psyche at work (the destructive forces of which we look at in Chapter Seven). When a dream manifests itself during the analytical process, it is always approached with great care, as it offers an opportunity to mirror back creative elements to the patient's consciousness deeply belonging to him or her.

Once again, Jung, making frequent use of spatial metaphors, highlights that:

> In the normal course of things, fantasy does not easily go astray; it is too deep for that, and too closely bound up with the tap-root of human and animal instinct. It has a surprising way of always *coming out right* in the end. The creative activity of imagination frees man from his bondage to the "nothing but" and raises him to the status of the one who plays. As Schiller says, man is completely human only when he is at play.

The reference to what Winnicott will theorise decades later is remarkable, and Jung proceeds to declare that his

> aim is to bring about a psychic state in which my patient begins to experiment with his own nature a state of fluidity, change, and growth where nothing is eternally fixed and hopelessly petrified.

> (Jung, 1931, pp. 45–46)

The contact of the consciousness with those aspects of the unconscious nature gives back hope, as it allows us to perceive the possibility of feeling that we are once again making progress/becoming.

Once more, it is not rational comprehension of the possibility of a way out of the "labyrinth of psychic discomfort" that is most useful during therapy, but rather contact by the consciousness with constellated symbolic content within the patient themselves, and with their emotional quantum, that is essential.

One of the means to allow contact with constellated unconscious aspects is thus to listen to what is presented in the dream theatre, when the patient remembers his or her dreams. Basically, this is the prospective function of dream activity, a concept frequently expressed in Jung's work, which can also be found in many recent works by analysts dealing with the manifold functions of the dream.

Renato De Polo, for example, states that the analyst, by listening to and understanding unconscious unrepresentable elements that the dream may bring to the surface, acts as a mind, able to represent them to the patient.[3] The action of containing and reflecting elements that cannot be processed implicitly, conveys the possibility that this can be done, with a desirable constellating effect.[4]

Likewise, Roberto Tagliacozzo asserts that a dream represents both the vital project of the patient and the opposing defences. He also states that this aims to set the stage for "a search for a solution and *a route other than repetition*". He expresses what the patient can do with their psychic material, which the analyst tries to help them make the best of and to transform this material into an "evolution in representability and thinkability" (Tagliacozzo, 1992, pp. 6–7; translated for this edition, italics added).

The neo-Freudian school declares that the dream process, with its plot, characters, places, situations, and the affects by which it is pervaded, represents "*the way* to a construction of the self" (Palmieri, in Bolognini, 2000, p. 260; translated for this edition, italics added) as well as a surprising way to "give processable shape to what the patient knows but knowledge of which does not seem to be available to them" (Roccato, in Bolognini, 2000, p. 412; translated for this edition); the latter quote allows us to recall that the sense of possibility (thinkability) belongs to the patient, although they may not consciously be aware of it.

In essence, the model of constellation of the archetype of Possibility can account for what, albeit in different terms, is implicitly described as the therapeutic factor at work in the clinical practice of other depth psychologies, particularly where dream interpretation is used with a prospective-transformative key.

At this point, we might ask whether our model has any heuristic value with patients with whom a journey similar to an individual analytical one is not possible, patients who do not remember their dreams and who have difficulty moving into a symbolic dimension.

The work of Carlo Zucca Alessandrelli lends itself well to answering this question. Indeed, he describes a group therapy experience, called GRF (Group for the Recovery of Functions), aimed at severe cases presenting alcohol and drug dependence problems, as well as a range of phenomena such as behavioural problems and narcissism.

The author claims that the transitional experience of the group,

> being part, together with other people, of a quest for meaning and value, for rediscovering the ability to give meaning, which one had come to consider impossible, and to see it recognised by others and to recognise it in others, kickstarts once again the transformative function and the self.
>
> (Zucca Alessandrelli, 2001, p. 334; translated for this edition)

From this quote, we can already see the defining elements of the model proposed here, namely the presence of a *significant relationship* (in this case, not only with the therapist, but also with the group, perceived as valuable), capturing an aspect of *unconscious possibility* belonging to the patient and of which their consciousness is not aware (rediscovery of the ability to give meaning, which they considered impossible), and the consequent jumpstart of *transformative and evolutionary potential.*[5]

The containment offered by the group, in this case, is certainly more effective than what is experienced in the relationship with the therapist alone. With the duly modified *setting*, a significant, intersubjective field is prepared, in which the archetype of Possibility (the transformative function, in the words of Zucca Alessandrelli) can be constellated.

Even within theoretical systems that wilfully ignore the unconscious psyche and use paradigms derived from cognitivism, in a broad sense, we can speculate that the constellation of the *daídalon* (or conscious awareness of unconscious potential, activated in the relationship with a significant figure such as the therapist) can trigger changes, in certain patients. Without the contribution of unconscious factors, it would be reasonable to believe that any subsequent therapeutic success would be temporary, at best.

A reflection of this nature could also shed some light on the phenomenon known as the "placebo effect". In the eyes of scientists, the latter is achieved through the blind trust of the patient in a therapeutic method, remedy, or drug, with no proven value, resulting in therapeutic success. However, little importance is given to such success, as it is not obtained through "good reasons", as Isabelle Stengers put it, the reasons of scientific rationality. But clearly, we can speculate that the remedy is truly effective, in some cases, as, by constellating the *daídalon*, it would benefit from unexpected transformative potential. In an attempt to stimulate broader reflections, in this comparison between models, we might include a very different, "alternative" method of healing, compared to those developed in Western culture.

Tobie Nathan writes about this method in his publications (1996; 2003) as "ethno-psychoanalysis". With a caustic and irreverent style, the French author is harshly critical towards Western psychiatric and psychotherapeutic thinking, which are seen as arrogant, with their attitude of supposed neutrality and "truth" over what illness, diagnosis, and treatment are. Nathan maintains that the Western world is a "single-universe" world, that of visible reality, which only science, in its various forms, is able to understand. In this world, madness is an illness which, like all illnesses, resides

> in the subject; in their psyche (according to psychoanalysis and its innumerable derived currents), in their biology (according to psychopharmacology), in the sediment of their personal history (existentialism), in the repercussions of their education (bioenergetics, therapy of Gestalt, transactional analysis).
>
> (Nathan & Stengers, 1996, pp. 17–18; translated for this edition)

In this single-minded society, the patient is referred to the expert, the scientist possessing knowledge, is isolated from the groups he or she belongs to, and is assigned to a diagnostic category, which is essentially a statistic group.

From a diametrically opposite perspective, "savage" societies are "multi-universe" societies. In such societies, there is not only visible reality but also invisible worlds, which manage to make their presence felt. In this environment, the expert him- or herself is the patient. It is he or she who is somehow in contact with the "other world", that invisible world of the spirits. In order to tackle psychic and physical discomfort, it thus becomes necessary to turn to the one who understands the spirits and their world: the healer, the shaman, the so-called "man of the secret". He does not investigate the patient, does not seek indications in him or her, does not make a diagnosis, but rather practises divination techniques to get into contact with the "other world", in order to understand the intentions of the supernatural being which has "caused" the illness and to have discourse with it. The healer does not deal with the patient but with the spirit world.

One consequence of this type of treatment is that the patient, far from being separate and isolated, perhaps pitied or stigmatised, is instead assigned to a group. He or she is an elected member of a particular group, characterised by uncommon properties. By doing so, Nathan maintains, the therapeutic techniques that the Western world would class as primitive "shift the focus: 1) towards the invisible; 2) from the individual to the collective; 3) from what is fatal to what is fixable/reparable" (Nathan, 1995, p. 25; translated for this edition). The latter statement is particularly interesting in the view put forward in this work. The words "fixable/reparable" suggest the essence of the clinical hypothesis that we are exploring, that in which the healer captures and implicitly reflects a sense of Possibility.

It is a real shame that Nathan had not read Jung's work extensively. The concept of "single-universe society" bears a close resemblance to the concept of excessive consciousness' one-sidedness (the attitude of primacy attributed to reason/rationality as a function of the ego) to the detriment of the unconscious dimension, and considered by Jung to be responsible for the break with the unconscious and the consequent psychic discomfort experienced by Western people. Jung also speaks of the "other world" and lauds its importance as the unconscious world, populated by figures and presences, complexes and archetypes, with a tangible effect on visible reality.

Although the definitions of symbol put forward by Jung and Nathan differ greatly, there are, however, several points of convergence between what Nathan describes and analytical psychology. In line with Nathan's model, described above, Jung also essentially shifts the focus from the visible to the invisible, considered to be intentional (the unconscious and its autonomous contents), from the individual to the collective (Jung is particularly effusive in this respect when talking about the unconscious), and from what is fatal to what is fixable/reparable (from causalism to prospective view). If the French author delved a little deeper than the widespread and inaccurate preconception of a "mystical Jung" and read the eighth volume of the *Collected Works* closely, for example, great would be his surprise at reading the description of a case of healing, in all respects similar to the many cases cited by him personally in his texts, seventy years later.[6] What was an enigma to Jung was, to Nathan, simply the effect of the operating method of the therapeutic system in multi-universe societies, and he does not bother to understand why they work, so long as they work.

How can we explain the numerous healings carried out using these types of methods, which are still in use in so-called "developing" societies today? Simply stating that they are mere superstitious beliefs would be one way to avoid confronting their indisputable effectiveness, and it would not be particularly scientific to declare what we cannot explain to be unreal, as is also the case with the tautological concept of the "placebo effect".

Perhaps the theory of constellation of an unconscious element can also be extended to what happens in the treatment carried out by healers in traditional societies. The witch doctor, through methods of divination, seeks a cause for the discomfort of the patient in supernatural presences. They are indeed the cause of the disturbance. But *you can have dialogue with them. You can escape* the labyrinth of discomfort and suffering.

The representation of an invisible world populated by beings who poke their noses into human affairs is totally accepted by collective culture but, obviously, this corresponds to the "unconscious landscape" of the patient, and activates a transformation which may take effect. According to Nathan, this happens even when the patient does not consciously believe in spirits, thus regardless of their conscious attitude.[7]

What is more important is that a sense of a possible way out is activated in the unconscious, and it must be pointed out that even in this case, this takes place within a significant relationship, the one with the healer. From the moment that "possible" does not mean "certain" in any way (see Chapter Eight), it is essential to note that the "cure" is still *Deo concedente*, as Jung would say, and this is also highly applicable to the cases studied by Nathan, examining situations in which the spirit which has allegedly caused the problem resists any form of dialogue.

The model of activation of the archetype of Possibility could thus be a common denominator, which can also be identified in forms of healing very different from those belonging to Western culture.

To conclude this chapter, we might just mention how important it may become to bear this model in mind during the diagnostic phase, when the patient arrives with some symptoms, and essentially wishes for a recovery of previous function. Given that the unconscious often "makes it own way", and that certain patients are better off *despite* going to a psychotherapist, it is however true that the analyst can play an essential role in facilitating dialogue with the unconscious that the patient is unable to successfully carry out on their own.

Archetypes, pre-disposals, constellate through an experience, thus it is through relationships that it becomes possible to promote their activation in some way. Even in forms of therapy that rely on the capacity of the unconscious to produce symbols independently (as is the case with Sandplay Therapy, for example) with minimal participation from the therapist, in terms of interpretations, reflections, and so on, it is still the case that the production of symbols always takes place *through* the relationship with the analyst, in their presence.

The therapist represents the guarantor of the possibility that the process will move forward in a constructive manner, offers him- or herself as a silent but ever-present observer, witness to a psychic event, which in solitude would not be necessarily individuative. If the analyst, with varying degrees of presence and guidance, either intervenes very little or actively guides the journey, he or she can promote constellation of the *daídalon*, but can also hinder it. The latter is what happens, for example, with an "incorrect" diagnosis, which does not correspond to the "unconscious landscape" of the patient. This can block off paths, which may lead to a "way out" of the discomfort and does not convey any perception of possibility.

At times, the theory to which the therapist is making reference can metaphorically create "walls and corridors in a labyrinth" which do not represent those of the patient, and prevent them following an individuative path.[8] Alternatively, the personal "labyrinth" of the therapist (in terms of their own unanalysed unconscious content, their own sore "knots" and unresolved problems) can overlap with those of the patient, leading to blind spots or dangerous collusions, in which both get lost.

In light of the fact that diagnosis requires a certain mental attitude, reading into what happens during the diagnostic process in the mind of the analyst could be a fruitful line of research, at which we can only hint here.

# PART III

## MIDDLE-EIGHT

## CHAPTER SIX

# Theory and ethics

E very theory of the mind is a more or less successful attempt, made by the conscious psyche, to describe the undescribable by definition: the psychic process.

Nevertheless, the immediate consequence of a theory of the mind is to define what is possible and what is not possible within a psychotherapeutic journey, as if it builds walls and paths; after building them, it becomes necessary to pass precisely from *there* and not from any other place, unless one breaks down the walls (as the unconscious often does, with symptoms and symbols).

Drawing the lines of a theory, thus, a theorist should remember to use pencil and eraser, so to say, in order to look back on what he or she has drawn and correct it, because defining what is possible and what is not, what is normality and what is pathology, is equal to stating what is "right" and what is "wrong".

Ethics must be clearly present in the mind of the theorist, because practical consequences of a theory have an immediate impact on the ethic dimension. A particularly rigid theory is thus in serious danger to break this dimension.

# PART IV

## DEVELOPMENT AND CLOSING CHORDS

## CHAPTER SEVEN

# Developing the theme—Possibility, Impossibility, and individuation

Discussing Possibility necessarily obliges us to take into consideration what may, upon first glance, seem to be its opposite: that is, the concept of Impossibility.

Archetypes, like complexes and the psyche in general, are thought to have polarity, and even in the case of Possibility, we are called upon to come face to face with the concept that contradicts it.

Even if one does not wish to credit the Jungian theory of opposites, clinical practice nevertheless forces us to look at the impossible: constellation of the *daídalon* seems simple, if only in words. Experience with patients shows us that the analyst very often finds him- or herself battling against unconscious forces with clear, destructive polarity. Coping with a negative therapeutic reaction, already identified by Sigmund Freud, and with strong resistances to change is extremely common, with neurotic patients as well.

We can find a heartbreaking metaphor for Impossibility in a short tale by the Swiss writer and dramatist Friedrich Dürrenmatt.

This metaphor is set in the Cretan labyrinth and is none other than the narration of the famous myth of Theseus, but told from the point of view of the Minotaur.

The son of Pasiphae, the wife of Minos, and a white bull sacrificed to Poseidon, the Minotaur, with a bull's head and a human body, after spending several years in a barn amongst the cows, was dragged into the labyrinth built by Daedalus to shut him in, a labyrinth whose walls Dürrenmatt fancies to be made of mirrors.

In the darkness of night, the Minotaur finds himself seeing his own image, endlessly reflected, wherever he turns. Every movement of his powerful body triggers infinite identical movements, and like a child observing the world with no self-consciousness, although initially scared, the creature slowly begins to rejoice, as he registers the consonance, the synchrony of movements, the sounds that he produces, and the movements which the infinite images reflect with his own senses.

The Minotaur—the author clearly stresses—finds himself being solely unconscious, "in a world full of crouched beings, never knowing that this being was him" (Dürrenmatt, 1987, p. 9; translated for this edition). Instead of finding beside him a warm being which *sees* him, mirrors him, cares for him, and meets his needs, the man-bull is tragically reflected, in the absence of another of his own kind, by cold, mirrored walls.

He experiments with movements and expressions, which are returned accurately but not embodied, and he can do nothing other than remain on the level of senses, perception, and the experience of affects. All that he can reasonably register is the simple correspondence of images and movements, from which he takes pleasure—a pleasure at existing and moving which can also be seen in newborns.

Suddenly, amongst the thousand images dancing with him, he becomes aware of an immobile figure, indeed a thousand immobile figures beside those dancing, and he stops for a moment.

In the labyrinth of mirrors, a terrified girl is staring at herself infinitely surrounded by reflected monstrous creatures, knowing that only one is real. The monstrous creature understands (although this verb may be too advanced to describe the embryonic awareness of sensation) that this is a sort of variation, and his curiosity is somehow piqued. So he begins to follow this figure which is different from the others, and the figure flees, in a whirl of images of minotaurs pursuing and girls fleeing. When he reaches her and touches her, it is another unknown sensation: she is not glass—smooth, cold, and hard, infinitely reflecting his image—but flesh, warm flesh, bathed in sweat, trembling, and panting.

The Minotaur dances, and drags the terrified girl into a frenzied dance, but instinct, pure oblivious instinct, means that he kills her as he embraces her, as he holds her close to him, in his excitement. The Minotaur cannot know what death and life are, as he has no consciousness to distinguish them. He is purely sensory, pure emotion, and he cannot see that following his own force and his own excitement, the naked body of the girl now lies lifeless on the ground.

He touches it, moves it, licks it, but it remains still.

He stands, and sees minotaurs standing, and motionless bodies of girls lying on the ground, everywhere.

As in the classic plots of Greek tragedies, the Minotaur feels the terrible guilt of the unconsciousness: not knowing, the unconsciousness of oneself and one's own actions makes him guiltlessly guilty.

You cannot help but think of the words of Jesus on the cross as he says "Forgive them, Father, for they know not what they do", thus indicating the crux of the human situation, in lack of consciousness, from which terrible consequences derive.

The Minotaur, an animal void of consciousness, only unconscious psyche, falls asleep, and dreams, and the dreamlike images depict his desire, show him playing, chasing, holding a girl close and loving her.

When he wakes from the dream, among the infinite images of himself waking, he sees another "new" image, that of a young man, this time, a figure in some ways similar to the girl, and he is gripped by a less eager, less sexual curiosity, that drives him to chase it, to play, trying to be less forceful this time, so as not to make it still and motionless.

The Minotaur, happy to have found another (although not clearly perceived as one other than himself) to play with, dances and circles all day long near this other, in the light of the sun.

But when the shadows fall once more, he finds himself with a sword in his chest, and beholds a thousand images of a Minotaur with a sword lodged in its chest, and feels a pain which he does not comprehend, and he is drenched in a warm liquid which he does not understand. He simply feels instinctively that this being does not love him, in the first simple distinction between good and bad.

And shortly other beings like him arrive, hand in hand, girls and young men and "the man-bull had the impression that all of humanity, if he could understand this concept, was swooping down upon him to destroy him", writes Dürrenmatt, in his dry prose (Dürrenmatt, 1987, p. 43; translated for this edition).

The feeling that invades him is one of hate, hate that the animal nurtures for the most dangerous and cruel of all the creatures which ever walked the earth, capable of immense creations, and at the same time, even greater destructions.

As the young people are already senselessly celebrating the death of the monster, and dancing around the body of the great animal, forgetting that they are lost in the labyrinth, the Minotaur, quivering with rage, suddenly gets up, attacks them and destroys them, reducing them to a heap of limbs, and bodies, and blood, and screams, and pain, raging on until their deaths, greeted by the rising sun and the flight of greedy vultures circling in the sky above the labyrinth.

And the Minotaur finds himself alone once more, accompanied only by the cold images of a thousand lonely minotaurs. He now violently hurls himself towards the images watching him, and breaks the glass of the mirror, finding another angry, seething image watching him. And he lashes out again, in blind rage, doomed to have as his interlocutor an Other who is not an Other, who is only the image of himself, who cannot give him right to existence, nor offer him that difference which would slowly permit him to distinguish between himself and other than himself.

The unreal other cannot constellate any possibility. The unreal other can give him no name because, in turn, it has no name.

Differentiation between consciousness and unconscious cannot take place in Absence: the Minotaur, with no reflection, *revérie*, the care of a good-enough other, is doomed not to emerge as a conscious subject.

Once more, the dream world depicts his deepest desire—universal and archetypal, one might say—of a relationship, involving an I and a You:

> He dreamed of a language, he dreamed of brotherhood, he dreamed of friendship, he dreamed of safety, he dreamed of love, closeness, warmth and, at the same time, he knew, as he dreamt, that he was abnormal, one who would never be granted a language, never brotherhood, never friendship, never love, never closeness, never warmth.
>
> (Dürrenmatt, 1987, p. 61; translated for this edition)

The desire to be a man is denied by the dream itself, by the bitter proto-awareness of never being able to become fully human.

Ariadne, holding her red thread in her hand, finds him still asleep, whilst Theseus, donning a bull head to trick him, prepares to kill him.

When he wakes, perceptions and sensations alert him once more to the presence of another being, very similar to the now familiar images reflected, but not perfectly in sync with his own movements.

After the natural initial diffidence, the bull-man explodes once more into a cry, a cry of real joy, because he realises in his heart that he is no longer the only one, the outcast, the lonely one, the prisoner.

There is another Minotaur, there is no longer just I but also You, and the Minotaur dances, dances with joy, and throws himself at this You with open arms, trusting he has found a friend, as he meets the dagger which strikes and kills him.

I find this short tale moving and afflicting, the tale of impossibility to be born psychologically, the dry narration of the impossible effort of the consciousness to emerge. The Minotaur is finally destroyed, just as he is deluding himself that he will be able to begin to exist in the eyes of an other.

In this story, I hear the painful echo of stories of other consciousnesses, other traumas, other impossibilities.

The archetype of Possibility, that "pre-disposal" to the possibility to develop a consciousness, needs to be activated within a significant relationship; in the absence of which it does not happen, and in the presence of early, acute, or ongoing trauma, it might reasonably be inhibited, or, to use a similar metaphor, constellate defensively in the opposite sense. What certain Jungian authors define as the ego–Self axis cannot be formed under traumatic conditions, unless in some deficient version, with a fragile ego complex, easily exceeded by a negatively polarised Self. The dynamic between ego and Self, between consciousness and content of the unconscious, which characterises the transformative process Jung has dubbed individuation, cannot take place, or rather, is opposed by tremendous psychic forces. In the unconscious (which, for Jung, is a continually transformative process, also through a relation to the ego, oriented in the sense of psychic completeness), Possibility is not constellated.

Freud, who, faced with the evident impossibility of healing certain patients, was forced to postulate the so-called "death drive", along with the libido, Eros, and vital energy, certainly struck upon a truthful aspect: the presence of antagonistic forces in every form of evolution, noticeable even in less seriously afflicted patients.

Other authors have suggested many definitions, ranging from Fordham's "defences of the Self", to Fairbairn's "internal saboteur", to Guntrip's "antilibidinal ego", to Seinfeld's "bad object", and so on, in an attempt to name the diabolical forces (which split, as indicated by its Greek etymology *dia-bàllein*), which oppose the individuative journey.

Donald Kalsched talks about these antagonistic forces as the archaic defences of the Self. In his work, we can find further support for the hypothesis that constellation of the archetype of Possibility might represent an explicatory model of what happens when therapy heals. According to Kalsched, when, in therapy with patients who have suffered acute or ongoing trauma, the relationship with the therapist becomes "dangerously" good, and results start to become noticeable and significant, unconscious archetypal content is activated, representing the dark side of the Self. This side tends to destroy the newborn possibility of growth, often manifesting itself in the form of demonic figures, in dreams full of anguish. The author suggests that this is the explanation for resistance to healing and for the proposed negative therapeutic reaction, which led Freud to postulate the theory of the aforementioned death instinct.

Unlike Freud, Kalsched maintains that the demonic figures that appear in dreams to destroy any hope of change in the patient, just at the moment when they have made progress, are the representation in images of archaic and typical defence orchestrated by a primitive Self, aimed at preventing any repetition of the painful, traumatic situations in which the subject has previously suffered.

Unlike the Self in its creative pole (which should promote the individuation process, which manifests itself in the capacity of compensation of the unconscious for the unilaterality of the consciousness, and which allows us to view the symptom and discomfort prospectively, as failed attempts to heal), the Self described by Kalsched is influenced by early trauma, which leads to mobilisation of a wrong-headed/persistent and unmodifiable unconscious mechanism, which aims to prevent any significant relationship, seen as particularly dangerous. To avoid further traumas, this archaic Self ends up becoming the same ongoing traumatising factor, as it prevents the patient from engaging in any positive relational experience, and often puts him or her in situations that in some way repeat the original trauma.

Kalsched's text is very enlightening when beginning to consider the aspects that at first appear merely dysfunctional in a potentially positive light: the archaic Self is somehow trying to protect the subject, and from the clinical examples given in Chapter One and Chapter Four, we see that detecting this often leads to the opening up of new paths, allowing them a possible way out. Despite the alleged "unmodifiability" of archetypal content of this scope, Kalsched apparently believes that *it still seems possible* for therapy to proceed, by initially getting in touch with this archaic defensive content ("dialoguing" in some way with it), and thus bringing it gradually into the conscious dimension. Perception of possibility by the therapist is thus implicitly mirrored to the consciousness of the patient.

\* \* \*

Arabella, a woman a little over forty, came to me with serious depressive symptoms, which had appeared a few months earlier, following a break-up with a man described as very immature and unreliable, but who she couldn't quite put out of her mind. Because of this impossible relationship, she had even attempted suicide by taking a large quantity of drugs, but she was found in time, probably due to the fact that she had no real intention of taking her own life. In the past, she had often fantasised about relationships with famous people, in a constant search for affection and reflected value.

The predominant impression of the first few sessions was that Arabella had a history of unmet needs and humiliations which, as is often the case, unconsciously led her to have relationships with men who humiliated her and ignored her needs, men focused on themselves in a narcissistic and childlike fashion. Although they were clearly the "wrong people", even in her eyes, it was as if she was trapped and unable to get away.

She immediately began to come with very significant dreams, and in the course of our sessions, we dealt with various aspects of her life, rebuilding a narrative which allowed her to understand how much she had always needed an accepting relationship, in a much broader sense that she initially intended. In the sessions, she often acted like a child who was scared of being scolded for making a mistake.

After only five months of therapy, feeling decidedly better, she stopped coming, against my advice. My impression was that she had just begun a long journey, and we had barely touched upon certain unconscious content, thanks to her intense dreams. In my opinion, it was definitely too early to stop. Nonetheless, she stopped coming, very happy about the fact that in one of the last sessions, she had dreamed about living in a solid house, still to be furnished, certainly, but nice and comfortable, completely different from that fragile tent in which she had dreamed she lived at the beginning of therapy.

After around five months of silence, she called me to make another appointment. She spent the session reassuring me that she was doing very well, that she wasn't thinking any more about the past that had made her suffer, that she was able to be much more assertive in various areas, abandoning the submissive attitude that had always character-ised her. She was in a good mood—she seemed to have come to me essentially to update me on her progress and to thank me, and I felt her gratitude was sincere.

After another six months, Arabella turned up at my office once again, this time in the midst of a total crisis period. She ate very little, had begun to think obsessively about that relationship which had ended over a year before, and to have serious anxiety attacks that prevented her from leaving the house and getting about, unless accompanied. Just as in the first series of sessions, the patient feared that I would scold her and that I would think her a fool for having fallen into the same mis-takes as the recent past. My attempts to reassure her that I was certainly not there to judge her went ignored.

I reflected after that session that, as I had feared, the five months of therapy a year before had done little. Probably, in the lapse of time, I had come to represent what can be defined as "reflexive function", which at the time the patient was totally lacking, and thanks to this role, contact with me had made her feel better.

But not having had the time to interiorise the reflexive function her-self, she had only drawn as much benefit from therapy as was possible in such a short time.

Arabella did not turn up to the next session. Instead, she came the following week, bringing this dream, which had really struck her:

> My brother and I are in a two-storey house, a basement, like your office, Doctor, and a ground floor. We (my brother and I) live on the floor above. Everything was lovely there, the food was good. However, on the lower floor lived other people, including two in particular, as if it were me and my brother with a different appear-ance, dead people, eating rotten meat.
>
> Going down to the lower floor, I would say to them "come up, it's better at our place", but they stayed there. They said that they

were used to eating like that, for them it was normal. The girl who answered was me, but she looked oriental, of another race, and was eating rotten meat, with maggots, a disgusting thing.

My brother (maybe) said "Don't push them". The place was just the opposite of what was on the upper floor, and me and my brother left.

The dream happened the night before the skipped session. The house reminded her vaguely of her grandparents' house, where there was indeed a dark cellar where you went down stone steps, a place that had really frightened her as a child. This dream seemed to represent a "world above", light and comfortable, where the food is good, compared to an underground world, built with darkness, where there are living dead, another "her", and another brother, Shadow figures, so to speak, the reverse of the world of light. In this place, "she" has oriental features, which often for a Westerner refers to an unknown, mysterious, and unconscious dimension, far from the ego.

The image of being content with eating rotten food reminded me of her being content with "rotten relationships", which were not satisfying, destructive, and she was perfectly able to recognise the analogy of begging affection from those who denied her it, as if in turn, she was now accustomed to feeding herself rotting food.

In my opinion, the dream illustrated the situation in which the patient found herself at that specific time very well, but it also seemed to represent an invitation to dialogue with that underground world, which she clearly needed to do. More specifically, there was presumably a part of the patient that wanted to dialogue with the "dead" and which, in fact, in the dream, invited them to come up to the upper floor, the world of light of the consciousness. But at the same time, there was another part, represented by the older brother, which was telling her to let it go and come up, leaving that deathly, isolated, and separate world behind her. Living only on the upper floor allowed her to feel good enough and to function for a bit (as was the case in the first block of sessions), but ignoring the lower floor, where the dead make do with eating putrid meat, exposed her to the cyclical risk of feeling bad, particularly when it came to relationships, broadly speaking.

Again, Arabella skipped the next session, stating generic family reasons, which turned out to be serious anxiety attacks, so intense that she was unable to take the metro to get to my office. Worried by this intensification of somatic symptoms, I suggested that she get in touch with a psychiatrist colleague of mine.

In the next session, she talked more extensively about these symptoms and revealed that this was something she had had for many years. She hadn't made any mention of it in the previous block of therapy, and the patient announced that, in her opinion, the panic would pass when she was calmer and with a partner. It was pretty clear that the anxiety could be linked to serious attachment problems, in the case of a not very reassuring family environment. Unfortunately, after going just once to the psychiatrist colleague for pharmacological support along with our sessions, the patient didn't come back, stopping therapy once and for all.

This fragment of a case allows us to illustrate a situation in which, despite the dreams making reference to a possible dialogue with unconscious aspects, the forces opposed to the analytical process have clearly prevailed.

The dream in itself depicted a feeble attempt at contact, followed, however, by a return to the upper floor, with the intention of ignoring the needs, and even the very existence, of those unconscious characters. Also, the somatic symptom seemed to prevent access to a psychic dimension, in primis not allowing the patient to leave the house and come to sessions.

Despite a relationship with me characterised by a rather too positive exchange (in the first period of therapy, the patient was trying to be "the good patient", was talking to me as if I were a kind parent, even if potentially judgemental and devaluing, and in the gap between sessions, she sent me an acquaintance of hers as a patient, speaking very highly of me), and despite a series of dreams which showed the activation of unconscious content, and which began a dialogue with the unconscious, constellation of the *daídalon* did not take place. Resistance and fears prevailed, and the patient gave up on the sessions, as indeed the dream itself foresaw.

In cases like Arabella's, one gets the feeling that, despite potential for change, perception of a possibility can be absolutely terrifying. Ambivalence towards the therapeutic journey is to be expected in any situation, but whereas with some patients, despite "being between Scylla and Charybdis", progress is made in an individuative sense, with others you reach a point where the defensive aspects opposing possibility prevail. It can be expected for this to happen to an even greater extent with more seriously ill patients, such as psychotics, who, to use Jungian terms, have an extremely fragile ego complex exposed to the influence of overwhelming unconscious elements.

In a patient of this kind, we can assume that there have been serious deficits in the journey leading to construction of the ego. As a result, the psychic economy is calibrated on balances which, from a "healthy" mind point of view, are dysfunctional, but which, in psychosis, primarily serve a homeostatic function. Trying to impose upon a seriously ill patient an operating model that does not belong to them is equivalent to forcing a map onto their "unconscious landscape" that is not theirs, which does not correspond to it.

In this respect, Salomon Resnik's description may be enlightening, as he uses spatial metaphors to illustrate a fundamental point of passage, where the patient finds themselves on the brink of two different worlds: that of their psychotic reality, delusional and hallucinated, aimed at protecting them from the anguish of disintegration of the ego, and that of non-pathological reality, in which, however, they must give up their omnipotent grandiosity.

The loss of delusion brings on a state of narcissistic depression, and the experience of change in an evolutionary sense is seen as catastrophic. In a way, healing translates into abandoning the ability to transform reality in a delusional way.[1] It seems that, in some cases, a psychotic is unable to tolerate the possibility of pleasure or of a moment's happiness, which is an intrinsically fragile, unstable, and very difficult to control condition. He seems to prefer to live in a world of pain, which can at least be controlled, as well as being very easy to obtain and maintain.

In this kind of situation, talking about constellation of the archetype of Possibility, as we have described it previously, is rather difficult, as, first, we can suppose that there have been serious obstacles in the course of construction of the ego complex, and second, because the psychosis itself forces the concept of Possibility to expand in directions other than what we might call a neurotic point of view.

\* \* \*

Fabian is a patient I have been seeing for around a year and a half. He came to me with a sexual problem: he wasn't able to get an erection sufficient for him to have full intercourse.

The diagnostic consultation discussions showed a decidedly schizoid personality.

At the age of forty, Fabian, the son of extremely wealthy entrepreneurs, lived with his parents, and worked for the family business, had never had a stable and lasting relationship, had had his first sexual intercourse rather late, aged twenty-five, with a prostitute, and his relationships with friends seemed rather poor.

Other than work, Fabian's life revolved around lonely evenings watching films on demand, and nights out with "friends", on which he consumed large quantities of alcohol, took cocaine, and went off with prostitutes, with whom he experienced both difficulty getting an erection and premature ejaculation.

The patient brought me basically no dreams, and seemed to have little ability to symbolise, remaining on a very pragmatic, concrete level where he essentially asked for behavioural advice. When, for instance, I found myself telling him that drugs and alcohol might be worsening his sexual problems, he stopped drinking, taking cocaine, and even smoking overnight, managing not to fall back into his habits for several months.

I was mainly trying to help him to identify feelings and emotions, to connect them, and bring them together, to learn a sort of relational "ABC"—all tasks that seemed totally new to him. Later in therapy, I also helped him to disentangle the great difficulties of a very conflicted and fragile relationship that he had taken up with a rather problematic girl.

I reckon that together we took, in essence, a journey of support, but I asked myself at length whether the therapy was really useful and why. I have never had the impression that a sense of possible change had been constellated, in the sense described in these pages. In the case of Fabian, it was about measuring this with a different concept of possibility. It was somehow possible for him "to be" differently within the structure of his personality; knowing how to handle his own feelings better, without imposing objectives which did not belong to him, how to be more extrovert, confident, and no longer inclined towards abusive behaviours. Imposing a different operating model did not seem a viable road at all. Nevertheless, it was possible to handle certain aspects of his life better. When therapy ended, by mutual agreement, the sexual problem, however, was still present, as at the start of treatment.

With this clinical example in mind, we must ask ourselves what it means *to heal*. In Fabian's case, could we have talked about healing if the problem of failing to get an erection had disappeared? Because the symptom was still there at the end of therapy, did I fail in my duty? Does the fact that he gradually managed to gain even the slightest ability to feel emotions and to recognise them, unlike the start of therapy when everything was described without affective tone and only on a pragmatic level, represent a conquest? To use the labyrinth metaphor, did he find a way out? Could I, as the therapist, have done more?

I think it is rather difficult to reason it out in general terms of "healing", as we would need to define the perspective we are moving from: the operating model that our society endorses in every field is very broad when applied to the psyche. Within this model (that of the society of technology), if something has a functional problem at any point, the causes of the problem are identified, understood, and resolved, and the previous function is restored.

From such a perspective, to which Western medicine subscribes, mental discomfort is an expression of a failure to function, which has causes. Once clarified and removed, one can simply return to the previous state of functioning.

The psyche does not, however, seem to be so docile as to be locked up within the narrow confines of the medical or technical model.

Starting from the supposed existence of a conscious psyche which represents just a small fragment of a much larger unconscious psyche, the symptom and the discomfort play the role of epiphenomena which refer to one another, an opportunity for expansion of the conscious psyche to embrace unknown areas of oneself.

Using the metaphor of the labyrinth, it is thus essential to highlight that "finding the way out" is not necessarily equivalent to "healing", in the sense of disappearance of the symptom and restoration of the previous level of functioning. From time to time, "finding a way out" may mean many things, such as: increasing the dignity of one's own existence; living with one's own deficits; integrating parts of the unconscious; disengaging oneself from the negative effects of an autonomous complex; increasing one's level of freedom; reconstructing an affective narrative; getting in touch with aspects of the self that have been denied the opportunity to manifest themselves; managing the tension between opposing content and transcending it; recovering or beginning a symbolic capacity; promoting the thinkability of primary emotions; and perhaps many others too.

Given the link between the word "healing" and models of the mind that are difficult to combine (due to the fact that they reduce the mind to a mere blocked mechanism to be fixed), we may turn to the concept of individuation, which Jung suggested was the ultimate purpose of human life, and also of the therapeutic practice of analytical psychology. Moving from the initial definition of individuation, contained in *Psychological Types*, as a process of the individual aiming to distinguish them from the collective psychology and from its norms, Jung veered towards a decidedly more complex concept, in the sense of embracing (*complector*) a set of equally contradictory aspects.

The ultimate goal of the individuation process is claimed to be to reach psychic completeness, the alchemic *Unus Vir*, the in-dividual (non-divisible), the Total and complete Man. The ego, wrongly considered to be the centre of the psyche, when relating to the unconscious (to be understood as an adjective) discovers that it is not "master of the house" but rather "subject to" (*sub-jectum*) something much vaster of which it is part. The Self (considered by Jung as the psychic wholeness which includes the unconscious and consciousness, thus the ego too) should, for the purposes of the process, take the central role, in the overall personality, the position that was initially occupied by the ego.

The concept of Self is rather contradictory and difficult to define. It is the Beginning (that which precedes the ego and from which it originates), and the End, or rather the ordered totality of the psyche which includes conscious and unconscious in creative tension; again, it is the same ordering principle of psychic life, an archetype promoting development and producing symbols, in a dynamic relationship with the consciousness.

The individuation process can thus be better captured not through rational explanation but through symbolic images (the symbols of the Self), such as those found in myths and fairy tales, or those Jung illustrated in his extremely dense description of the *Opus*, that immense metaphor for spiritual development which alchemy has refined over the course of centuries of initiatory knowledge. The individuation process would be the result of the dynamic relationship between the ego and the unconscious, aimed at resolving antinomies through the transcendent function, to achieve a complete psychic unit, full expression of the Self.

According to Jung, this process begins with the dissolution of the Persona,[2] that shell which we present to the world, the façade, the role imposed by the process of adaptation to the society in which we live. The demands of the collective require that we wear this and give up a more authentic, but not directly demonstrable, subjectivity; nevertheless, the Persona is essential to civil human interaction. Although it is true that, on the one hand, this can restrict the more authentic individual personality, it is also true that it represents the necessary "through road" to interact with the world.

The problem is that often the ego identifies completely with the Persona. This happens when an individual believes that they are solely their role, unaware of their more genuine and profound nature. The awareness that the Persona is just a "mask", albeit certainly useful and part of us, but which also covers up other life-giving aspects of our being, is the *conditio sine qua non* of a journey of self-awareness.

Individuation could thus justifiably seem to take the lead from the critical integration of the Persona (recognising the use of interaction between the self and the world, without coinciding with it), and from the subsequent discovery in oneself of other psychic content, *in primis* the Shadow, that set of aspects of oneself that has been repressed, because it is deemed unacceptable by the world around, and over time by oneself.

But in light of what has been presented so far, it would be more correct to anticipate the beginning, and consider that the individuation process starts with the gradual emersion of the consciousness and the ego complex from the undifferentiated sea of the unconscious.

In human beings, there exists a predisposition to develop a consciousness and an ego complex more differentiated from that which we can assume is held by more evolved mammals. Jung may be referring to this when he talks about the archetype of the Self which promotes development of the ego, and somehow guides this development in the course of an individual's existence: advisedly, thus, the first step of the individuation process is the birth of the ego, as this cannot be maintained in the absence of the latter.

The development of consciousness, an event of enormous scope, which has taken millions of years of evolution to come to light in the history of humanity, is related to birth of the ego in the individual history of each human being. The latter corresponds to the violent separation initiated by the birth of the consciousness which, distinguishing, capturing the differences, is emancipated from the undifferentiated sea of the unconscious. The ego escapes the violence of the undifferentiated Self from which it emanates, with an equally violent separation, as attested to by many stories of origin, including those from the Bible.

The birth of the consciousness thus places the human being, unique amongst all animals, in contrast with the Self, the undifferentiated, beginning a rending conflict between opposites.

All of this takes place in the individual story of each one of us, in the process of emersion of the ego complex, but this can take place only and exclusively with the help of another human being who has, in turn, developed an ego sufficiently differentiated from the Self, and who gives right to existence, constellating the Possibility. A relatively solid ego complex requires activation of this "pre-disposal" which, as we have already said, operates at different levels, and not as an "all or nothing" phenomenon.

Although the Self is seen as the driving motor of the individuation process, this alone would not be able to initiate the process of emergence of the consciousness. If, as Jung says, individuation is the dynamic process of an ego which integrates the content of the unconscious, giving up the central position which it believes it occupies, it is clear that there cannot be an ego in contrast with the unconscious without the *presence* of someone who has authorised its existence and allowed its development.

So what we have dubbed *daídalon* could be used as a bridge between the Self and the birth of the ego, at that moment in an individual story when the relationship with other significant conscious–unconscious systems constellates it.³

The fact that an archetype of the Self which promotes the development of an ego can exist, does not at all shape an existence determined by unvarying and metastoric factors; this same development can only take place in the unique and unforeseeable story of that single emerging individual, in relationships with individuals who are in turn unique and inimitable, immersed in a specific collective culture and a language.

Archetype and possibilities, opposites in tension, blend together, and are not mutually exclusive, exactly as the existence of seven unvarying notes and five sharps do not pin down the music to an unalterable determinism in any way, and have not impeded the infinite possibilities of making music which have existed for centuries.

It is absolutely true that individuation is unthinkable outside of the category of Possibility, what is offered by the meeting of unique historical elements, which bring to life an inimitable life story.

To state that individuation begins with the emergence of the consciousness from the undifferentiated, with the essential contribution made by the caregivers who authorise this process, constellating the Possibility, makes the events surrounding the birth of the consciousness crucial, without falling into another determinism, through which the individual historical events which happen to the subject during childhood become *the* factor which promotes development, in accordance with certain foreseeable directions. It is the experience of many therapists, instead, to find themselves faced with patients whose terrible traumas and painful experiences have not managed to extinguish a yearning for development and have not prevented them from possible evolutionary journeys.

Once the consciousness emerges from the undifferentiated, as the individual gradually develops all the functions which belong to the ego complex, the relationship with external reality contributes somehow to create the so-called autonomous feeling-toned complexes, whilst the relationship, or rather the tension, between the consciousness and the entire unconscious psyche is configured as the main antinomy between opposites which defines existence, and gives the psychic energy a *raison d'être*.

It is on this contradiction that the consciousness is torn, as much as this evolves to a high degree of differentiation, and that the transcendent function of the symbol is built, aiming to bring the opposites together in a transformative synthesis, which overcomes them, although they remain as such. Symbolic activity as well, similarly to the individuation process, cannot do without an ego to capture the symbol in this way.

From this point onwards, the individuation process can unfold through a series of confrontations between the consciousness and the content of the unconscious, primarily, according to Jung, the Persona and the Shadow, and by means of the personal and collective psychic content which constellates in unique and personal patterns, in every single individual *en route* to their own complete, unique personality. A truly transformative confrontation takes place whereby the ego complex does not succumb to the unconscious. The individuative path becomes possible in the balance between destiny and history, where the individual uniqueness of the ego of each of us is found.

Everyday clinical practice with seriously ill patients may fully contradict the idea of a necessarily evolutionary individuative process, activated by a transcendent, a-historical Self, which guides seamlessly towards the composition of opposites and the creation of the totality.

From the undifferentiated Self, we reach an ego complex through the action of the archetype of Possibility constellated in a significant relationship. Then, according to Jung, various scenarios begin: the consciousness can hyper-differentiate itself and break off the relationship with the unconscious, unilateralising itself; the unconscious will seek to compensate for this one-sidedness with activation of content which often leads to symptoms; or a fragile consciousness can be held hostage by autonomous complexes, concretion of memories, images, and affects born of the relationship with external reality, which drastically reduce the levels of freedom; the consciousness can even be invaded and overcome by archetypal content, in the face of which it is unguarded and is lost in psychotic reality; or still, the consciousness can integrate unconscious content which it gradually finds, remaining active and strong, although giving up its own central position.

Jung looked at the individuation process in its advanced phases, managing to make use of the immense imaginal and symbolic range offered by alchemy. The process of continuous transformation of the unconscious in relation to the consciousness towards psychic completeness seemed to him to be the same process decribed in alchemic books. In different terms and with less awareness, alchemy's *ars regia* aimed at the same goal of completeness: the *Opus* had to start with the *prima materia* (the undifferentiated primordial substance) going through various processes of transformation, until reaching the *conjunctio oppositorum*, the *hieros gàmos*, the chemical matrimony between King and Queen, the *lapis*, all seen by Jung as symbols of the Self. But couldn't the maker of the *Opus*, the alchemist, without whom nothing could be achieved, realistically represent the ego complex itself?

Jung devoted less time to exploring the phase that starts with the appearance of the ego complex, but there have been many theorists and analysts in the world of depth psychologies who have dealt with this over the subsequent years (for instance, the English school founded by Fordham, to which this work may contribute in an integrative sense).

Different models of the mind employ different terms and metaphors to express the ups and downs of the emerging consciousness, but the model of constellation of the *daídalon* in a significant relationship which opens up to symbolic life seems to be a concept able to connect Jungian thinking with that of other analytical schools of thought, and could become a heuristic tool of some clinical use.

## CHAPTER EIGHT

# Closing chords—Possibility and Limit

On closer inspection, it seems clear that, over the course of its history, Western society has ended up repressing the concept of the Limit. As the repression is posed as an unconscious mechanism which intervenes to distance particularly painful and feared content from the individual's consciousness, moving the concept to a collective level, we can assume that Western society, nowadays in particular, greatly fears the Limit, and neutralises the resulting distress and discomfort by keeping it outside of the conscious horizon of its members.

Confronting the Limit would immediately require questioning the idea of scientific and technological "progress" which has taken root over the last two hundred and fifty years, since the Industrial Revolution.

The Greek myth of Prometheus, who steals fire from the gods to give it to men, clearly highlights that the beginnings of technology for mankind coincide with a theft, a criminal action, and that the direct consequence for having breached the limit is the terrible punishment suffered by Prometheus, when he is chained to a rock.

Some millennia ago, in the unconscious of humanity, there was the awareness of the risk that one ran in breaking the eternal rules of Nature. But, over the course of the history of development of the consciousness, humankind seems to have breached the limit, without any longer paying heed to the warning of the myth. A detailed description of the process that has led human beings to the conquest of technology, to the point of being dominated by it, can be found, for example, in Umberto Galimberti's works.

With little knowledge of how to soar to the heights of philosophy, we shall limit ourselves to considering how the scientific and technological impulse that has led man to (apparently) dominate Nature, ransacking it, and shaping it according to his needs, goes hand in hand with repression of the Limit, with all the tragic consequences resulting thereby, both on a collective level and on an individual psychic level.

Many people think of progress in primarily positive terms, first because they are part of that minority of human beings on the planet who benefit in some way: increased life expectancy, medical cures that have put paid to many illnesses which plagued humankind for centuries, access to (limited) food and water resources, owning a house, private means of transport, a tourism and leisure industry, and new information technologies are, in fact, the prerogative of the few, when considered on a global level.

Second, we are led to see, in the foreground of technical and scientific progress, the positive aspects only if we remove those enormous negative ones for which we all pay a price (unlike the benefits, the damages are democratically distributed amongst all human beings). These negative effects, in our opinion, are essentially three: the first is represented by the gap—not to mention the fracture—between technical and scientific progress, which has increased at frightening speeds over the course of just a few decades, and the psychic progress of human beings, which is significantly slower; the second by the current independence of technology from humankind, which involves a break with ethics ("everything that can be done, must be done",[1] without any consideration of the consequences), and a switch in roles whereby humankind, politics, and economy are in fact at the service of technology and its continuance; the third by the physical removal of the waste resulting from technical production, which is not much in sight of those who benefit from the technologies, but mostly swept under the rug of the third world (which, it must be noted, is still part of just one world: ours).

Planet Earth is a closed and therefore limited system: this offers the life forms which inhabit it a defined environment, as well as potential resources that are rather limited in quantity. But the idea of constantly increasing "progress" prevents us from considering this limit, the physical limit of the planet on which we live. Thoughtless consumption of resources crossed the line of sustainable balance some time ago, and the unlimited enjoyment of raw materials, seas, forests, and lands (often made possible by direct exploitation of the underprivileged people of the world) is irreversibly altering the eco-biological and climactic balances of the entire planet.

The specific case of fossil fuels, the true engine behind the enormous technological development in the twentieth century, is emblematic. Kurt Vonnegut, in his typical cutting and ironic prose, compares oil to a drug on which we are all dependent to make every element of our lives in this post-industrial society function. Despite this observation, we are constantly encouraged to buy cars, tempted to satisfy the "need for freedom and independence" which they promise, whilst simultaneously *de facto* denying us it.

A reasonable consciousness should see that the closed system naturally involves limitations and that eternal "progress" is impossible, particularly if it is based on a profound imbalance between distribution, consumption, and waste. To those who maintain that scientific progress is a rational concept, it would be interesting to ask what is rational about the fact that discovering atom fission has led to the proliferation of weapons capable of destroying the planet, not once but several thousands of times over, and that this absurdity is constantly reiterated by the arms race, which is by no means in decline.

To see to what extent the idea of unlimited development circulates on a daily basis, we can also use advertising communication, the distinctive characteristic of "civilised" society over the last century, as a litmus test.

To stay on the topic of fossil fuels and the car industry, it is useful to reflect on the fact that a modern metropolis is generally invaded every day by millions of vehicles, often with only one person on board, which inexorably consume almost unheard of quantities of that oil which is running out, whilst levels of atmospheric pollution often greatly exceed those set by European regulation. Collective removal of the Limit means that nobody thinks of giving up using their own vehicle, whilst advertising invites people to buy new cars, presented as a free means of expressing oneself and one's personality; even car manufacturers have branded their vehicles as SUVs (Sport Utility Vehicles), which in a society that considered the Limit would not even be produced, due to their greater consumption and increased risk in the event of an accident.

An interesting anecdote took place some years ago when the public transport company in Milan, my home town, went on strike without warning. The apocalyptic scenes that resulted were endless queues of vehicles at absolute gridlock on every street, lanes crammed with cars condemned to immobility for hours, and furious people trapped in massive congestion. Whereas the majority of people wondered angrily whether such a strike, which had damaged the entire city, was legal or not, it seemed clear to me that the surreal scenario of that day denounced an indisputable fact: Milan has "x" square metres of streets, a finite, limited number; when almost all of its citizens use their own cars at the same time, there is not the physical space to do so. The number of vehicles on the road is clearly higher than the figure expressed in square metres of the streets of Milan. But the repressed Limit means that nobody thinks even for a second about the original problem, or rather that this Limit has already been significantly exceeded, because taking note of it would probably lead to an immediate halt in car production. Instead, the economy, the field that seems to decide what is right and what is wrong in modern "democracies", shows a total blindness towards the concept of the limit, as it maintains production and sales of automobiles (and of many other so-called consumer goods) as an index of solidity and wellbeing, indicated by "development" indexes such as the gross domestic product.

Advertising, in the age of mass communication (which does not represent the world but rather *becomes* the world in which we live) specifically nurtures the idea of repression of the Limit, since almost any slogan can be reduced to the basic message "you can" or "it can be done", or, if you prefer, "there is no limit, whoever you are, you can": the examples of products or services which automatically allow you to step over the limits and access a world where you can do anything are countless.[2] In this message, a specific acceptance of the concept of Possibility is implicit, optimistic, and prone to sweeping aside obstacles and limits, thus reinforcing the repression: the affirmation "anything is possible" is commonly understood as a characterisation of the (near) certainty of success.

As this work talks extensively about Possibility, it is essential to clarify the deeper meaning of this concept, in order to avoid misunderstandings. The aim of the following reflections is to be able to show the very close relationship that exists between Possibility and Limit and to remove the misleading, omnipotent get-up that has been attached to the word "Possibility".

Probably the mass repression of the Limit, which characterises Western societies, can be highlighted by dealing with the greater limit to which every living thing must submit: death.

When a human being emerges from Nature, and opens up the world inaugurated by their own technical capacity, thanks to development of the memory, they are wrested from the horror of discovering that their ultimate destiny in life is death. Opening up meaning, which is granted to man, rather than animals, simultaneously leads to awareness of the total disappearance of any meaning brought by death.

Galimberti states that "Tragedy is therefore the constituent of man, whose memory, after having opened up meaning, reminds him that it has been opened up for nothing" (Galimberti, 1999, p. 76; translated for this edition). Death, the greatest Limit, the Unknown *par excellence*, because it escapes the conscious senses and remains silent on speculation of our thoughts, has always accompanied human beings on the short journey of personal life, and has been dealt with in very different ways over the course of history.

It is very interesting to note how, particularly in this historic period, this is summarily and widely repressed, as, however, Freud already noted in his "Civilisation and Its Discontents". The French historian Ariés illustrates how death was perceived between the Middle Ages and the twentieth century in the Christian West. The author's historical examination begins with an era in which man immediately knew that he was close to death, and this was essentially a public event, until our age, in which death is hidden *in primis* among the dying, and has become a private matter, in the double sense of intimate/non-public and deprived of a whole set of tools with which to face it and insert it into the journey of our lives.

In the Middles Ages, you could feel death coming: the individual knew they were near the end, and waited for it, often lying in their own bed, surrounded by masses of people, made up of family, relatives, and perfect strangers who just happened to be passing by. Nowadays, instead, the terminally ill are often kept in the dark as to the gravity of their condition until the end, in an attempt to protect them from anguish, and die alone, rarely at home but much more often in hospital, unconscious, perhaps hooked up to the machines provided by technology. The latter has become the true custodian of life and death, and determines life's extension or termination, according to current scientific parameters.

The rituals of medieval man, who could weigh up his existence on his deathbed, the good and evil he had committed, aspire to salvation of his soul, the rituals which allowed the dying man to take an active role (he might have swayed divine judgement towards forgiveness, given family members instructions to help his soul with masses and prayers, and, in turn, have the crucial task, once he reached the Beyond, of finding the dead, the ancestors, and asking them to watch over the living) make way, in our time, for a large and passive void of practices and meaning.

In the Middle Ages, death was accepted as part of life, a conviction maintained by Christianity, according to which true life began after that on Earth; what was most feared was sudden death in an accident or a violent act, as these events would have prevented them from carrying out all that was required by the dying ritual to save their souls. It is no coincidence that, in the collective imagination, the soul of one who has suffered a violent death cannot find peace, and roams the place where they lost their life. Nowadays, however, death is essentially repressed and we live our lives as if it did not exist.

When it does present itself, often through the great illnesses of our time (cancer, AIDS, epidemics of new viruses) or death in sudden circumstances, it is felt with a total lack of preparation and unspeakable pain: death is absurd and unfair, an atrocious wrong committed by a blind and arbitrary fate, which deprives us in an instant of all that we have painstakingly built.

The position that Heidegger dubs *forgetting of being*, or ignoring the indisputable fact of our mortality, losing ourselves in a present of objects, of day-to-day diversions, of distractions and padding/stupefaction, is totally understandable, because the other position, defined by him *awareness of being*, would imply acceptance of what it is, or rather our condition as mortals in search of meaning in a world which offers none, because it is like a river which we navigate on, at the end of which is the cliff of death.

Unlike early, ancient, medieval, and pre-modern man, who could in some way rely on myth and ritual to give some meaning to the experience as ancient as the universe, the dying nowadays do not know how to deal with their own deaths and no longer have rituals and myths to help them. Death has ended up in the hands of the "healthcare machine", which tries to make it as *correct* as possible, discreet, hidden as it is from view, which tucks it away and sometimes determines it, defining it and carrying it out.

As early as the 1950s, Geoffrey Gorer observed that the true "pornography" had nothing at all to do with sex, but rather death. It is death which is obscene and in fact is put "out of the scene" (*ob-scena*), not sex, which, on the contrary, is omnipresent and highly visible at every moment of our day, in magazines, billboards, films, and on every street.

The signs of death, in big cities, tend to disappear. The wake of the body of the deceased has become obsolete, as the death takes place, more and more often in a hospital; the hearse followed by a procession of loved ones, the band playing funeral marches, all the visible signs of death have been hidden from public view, and even the dark curtains in doorways are seen less and less, making way for a more discreet sign and a few black bows.

Statistics show that it is possible for a person to reach over thirty without ever having seen a dead body in person, an experience which only a few decades ago was completely ordinary. Children are "protected" from the shocking experience, certainly, of viewing a dead body but doing so takes away the essential part of this experience, which until a short time ago was considered normal.

Paradoxically, television and cinema show thousands of images of violence and death, even to children, in numbers and ways which, in the past, nobody would ever have seen in the course of their entire lives, but this scene is *elsewhere*, it is fiction and even when it depicts real situations, it is still distant and loses the characteristics of a real experience.

It is probable that the passion for horror and gore films which has characterised recent decades in particular is in some way the expression of an interest, turned morbid, in returning to seeing death up close, the same way that many people slow down near an accident. Distancing signs of death and its uncomfortable and cumbersome appearance thus characterise the civilisation of consumers in the twentieth and twenty-first centuries.

The psychic effect of repressing death is that of living an illusory brilliant and eternal life, although this is constantly threatened by depths of darkness, from which emanates a sense of worrying, growing uncertainty and insecurity. And, just as seriously, the disappearance of death from the horizon of life itself, preventing the individual from making peace with this inescapable experience, instead of giving them the possibility of living authentically, and thus fully, does not allow them to extract any meaning, as this would be found by taking into account the end, the Limit.

The most widespread mental illnesses in Western society, to simplify roughly, seem to have much to do with the idea of repression of the Limit, whether taking the form of narcissistic problems (omnipotence, involving denial of the limit and intolerance of obstacles) or depression (annihilation following the narcissistic wound, when they discover that the limit exists).

Despite believing myself to be sufficiently prepared by life experience and extensive reading into the subject, the day that I myself was handed a serious diagnosis, I was seized by a deep anguish, and I felt utterly a man of my time, a time oblivious of death. The unconscious, however, proved that it dealt with this issue much more than my consciousness in many dreams months before these events, and my mind "heard" the corresponding sound of an internal image—I might define it as an inner voice—speak the phrase "Death is a door, a door through which the body does not pass". I wrote down this phrase in a notebook and I observe it with curiosity, as if it were a strange creature, unknown to current classifications.

Ageing, too, is subject to a similar repression, as it represents another inescapable limit for every living thing. The second half of life, which Jung described as the phase in which the individual, after mastering their role in the outside world, could turn to their own inner world, to start a dialogue between unconscious content and the consciousness, is often kept at bay by the "society of eternal youth". Signs of ageing can be counteracted with an infinite range of means and techniques, such as cosmetics and plastic surgery and wardrobe, keeps those approaching old age tied to the dominant image, that of younger age groups.

Furthermore, advertising models are aimed exclusively at the young, and at activities which do not marry well with the requirements of an older person and continue to sing, like the sirens of Ulysses, of a world of pleasure and enjoyment in which anyone, even the elderly, *can* participate. Overexposure to sexual stimuli, addressed mainly to the male world, goes hand in hand with drugs to continue to function on an erotic level, in an attempt to keep at bay that certainly tiresome and rarely agreeable phase of life which is old age, conducting a massive repression of its positive qualities.

As Luigi Zoja highlights, the Latin word *senex*, from which the word *senator* derives, for example, an expression of the idea of maturity brought by experience, today appears rather in words such as *senile*, associated with a devaluation and loss of ability: more prosaically, one might say that the figure of the Old Sage has all but disappeared, to make way for that of the senile old fool.

"Old" is a negative quality: even a piece of music is already "old" after a few months, meaning to say that it is now *out*, far from the only point that has value, the eternal and young present. Only once a further, ever shorter, lapse of time has passed, does it transform from "old" to "classic", and can it once again be enjoyed in the eternal and young present, provided that the current fashion allows it to be so.

Thus, the elderly as custodians of historic memory, of sacredness related to being near to the *other* world, like children, the world of the ancestors, born and gone before, the elderly who can potentially have much to offer to the young, who might approach them for mysteries of existence, ruefully make way for the useless old man, unsuited to a world which changes too quickly, unable to work the ever-changing tools of technology, the old man who now has nothing to teach the young man about conscious reality, the only thing that counts in the eternal present.

Because this is the only reality for the collective consciousness, those approaching old age risk clinging to the present by any means that the consumer society offers them, and giving up on the future, freezing themselves in a psychic time that does not tick away.

We don't want to give a false, nostalgic impression of a time gone by in which the old person always represented a resource. This would be a certainly romantic and untruthful vision, as the roles of the sage, the witch doctor, the shaman, the guide, were certainly not the prerogative of all. But the substantial decline (with rare exceptions) of these types of figures in the panorama of societies of technology has been highlighted, a decline that accompanies denial of the very limit represented by ageing. In other areas, technology itself and its operating arm, science, have permitted the progressive extension of the limit.

To describe what took place at the end of the millennium, it is useful to consider the Jungian concept of excessive unilaterality of the consciousness, and the consequent break with the unconscious, which is thus at risk of activating to compensate for the conscious attitude. A widespread onesidedness of science, seen only for its enlightening aspects, poses the serious threat of a split with the Shadow sides, with fearful consequences.

Yet another example of denial of the Limit is represented by the proliferation of mobile phones nowadays: technology has created an unusual scenario in which everyone has the potential to be permanently connected. Being constantly connected is an induced need which previously did not exist but which, clearly, relies on common and rooted needs, as can be seen from the massive widespreadness of smart multifunctional phones.

If we skip a detailed analysis of Bauman where he talks about the passage from *relationship* (which "link" us to the other, which force a commitment, and expose us to suffering, due to the irreducibility of the other to our own needs, and moreover, to possible abandonment or betrayal by the other) to *connection*, (being much safer, as it is short and undemanding, and can be interrupted at the push of a button, with no responsibility towards the other person), the tragi-comedic irony of the statement "in the web, we are free" is stressed, perceptible to those who listen to the words and give them deep meaning.

If the invisible web of electromagnetic waves and internet as well, on one hand, represent connection and protection, at the same time it can ensnare, even trap, force, choke, like a spider's web. Paradoxically, these are exact opposites.

Leaving our mobile at home or, worse still, losing it now seems equivalent to losing our place in the community and, in general, our ever-present link which gives us a sense of existing. We exist if we are connected, otherwise we fall into a state of non-existence and solitude for the being.

Silence scares us, it is seen as empty, an abyss to back away from, to fill with words, often redundant and useless, but necessary to drown out its worrying presence.

The smart phone fulfils the purpose of making human beings feel that they belong and are connected and of nurturing the impression of being without limits: "free to navigate", "unlimited Internet"—these are widespread slogans in the society where "everything (revolves) around you".[3]

Jung was absolutely right when he maintained, in an age in which technology had not yet made the giant steps of the last forty years, that faced with a huge increase in scientific and technical knowledge, man remained essentially the same, on a primitive level of psychic evolution.

In the recurring news items, where teenagers gang rape a girl and film the entire thing on their mobiles, we can very clearly see the extent to which technology, which offers us a multifunctional tool, with which to navigate, to call, photograph, film, and listen to music, corresponds to a spiritually poorly evolved human being, still inclined to group violence, abuse of the weakest, looking for existence obtained through power over another, and through visibility. These characteristics have been identical for millennia, modernised only by the presence of the technological means, which allow us to satisfy the same needs as always: "to control the other", "to appease our own separation anxiety", "to exist if we are seen" in the places where the collective says to live.

Many modern-day authors, in various fields, have produced valuable sociological analyses and analytical works on these phenomena of the masses, and different visions of the world which translate into attempts to live lifestyles different from those proposed by the economic and technological model of the Western world are beginning to circulate.[4]

The purpose of these brief reflections on the eclipse of the concept of the Limit, as we said, is to clarify the meaning of the term "Possibility".

In a society like the Western one, in which economy, science, and technology ignore the Limit, and in which ethics are eclipsed in comparison, we could thus say that the prevailing and widespread message is that "anything is possible". It is possible to overcome old age and illness, to dramatically increase life expectancy; happiness, progress, enjoyment, consumption, and becoming "someone" are possible by owning certain objects and services; eternal happiness is a right afforded to anyone who follows the right technique, supplied by certain psychologies, and their emphasis on functioning, positive thinking, and wellbeing. All of this risks distorting the true meaning and scope of the word "Possibility".

The concepts of "possible" and "impossible" are often considered to be opposites whilst it would be much more accurate to counter "impossible" with "certain": on an ideal continuum which goes from "impossible" to "certain", it is the (transitional) area in the middle which represents the "possible". If the concept of "impossible" aims to indicate that something, an action, an event can in no way be realised, the opposite concept should be "certain", where the thing, the action, the event will certainly be realised. The concept of "possible" would instead be reserved for the vast range of situations in the middle in which the thing, the action, the event, could potentially happen, but it does not equal certainty, as it must reckon with a series of conditions, which make the occurrence more or less probable, and which represent limitations and either favourable or unfavourable eventualities, depending on the event.

In an attempt to clarify this thought, we can refer once more to the image of the labyrinth, from which many of the reflections in this work have originated. When we find ourselves in a labyrinth, finding a way out is not impossible, as we know that a way out exists. But this is not equivalent to saying that the way out is a certainty: the complicated network of passages may trap us forever in an agonising, fruitless search, or an encounter with the mythical Minotaur may spell death and annihilation. Finding a way out can be defined as a "possible" event, definitely, but in the precise sense that it can be found only genuinely confronting the Limit, or in this case the risks and dangers that the situation of the person in the labyrinth involves. The concept of Possibility expressed here is therefore closely linked to that of risk, it is the result of a tension between "certain" and "impossible" which the calculation of probabilities aims to deduce.

In a social context which suggests omnipotence at every level (technology, science, medicine, genetics, economics, psychologies, and so on) and which dramatically promotes the opposite, it is no trivial question to distinguish the "possible" from the "certain".

When we say "anything is possible", we give the false impression that "anybody can, there are no limits", glossing over any other meaning, and feeding a culture characterised by the easy and misleading optimism of positive thinking, which in fact excludes the Limit and the Shadow from our psychic lives. Indeed, it is this very confrontation with these dimensions that makes it truly possible to move forward on a journey of transformation, or along an individuative path. During this journey, the ego, which believes itself to be all-powerfully central, should be in the presence of the Limit, which has appeared from the unconscious and its products, as well as from the outside world and accept its resizing.[5]

The modern society of omnipotence, which believes in expanding the dominion of the ego and the consciousness into infinity, thus finds itself, on the one hand, totally unprepared for the compensation of the unconscious, and exposed to terrible psychic inflations (the rampant psychic imbalance and ever-deeper and more radical discomfort which dwells in the minds of those individuals who should be the happiest on the planet, those who live in the so-called society of wellbeing, in the first world, are perceived by all). On the other, this *Weltanschauung* is literally destroying the only world that we know, with the same smile on our lips the faces of the passengers on the *Titanic* probably wore as they danced, heedless of the danger, whilst the ship was sinking.

Returning to the image of the labyrinth, as it has been presented in these pages, the way out of all of this was previously the way in.

If the birth of the consciousness in the evolutionary story of human-kind immediately makes human being *tecnicus*, so to speak, and if tech-nology, from being a distinctive human element, becomes something that goes beyond our control and becomes independent, the turna-round to get out of the blind cycle that we have got ourselves into can only take place by means of technology. Humankind cannot stop being intrinsically technical. We cannot return to a natural state, because we have never been natural, but immediately became an *opus contra natu-ram*, right from that first flash of consciousness. Technology itself should be thus the way out of the tunnel of self-destructive inflation which pushes us. But technology, however, must be restored to the service of the ethics that matter at the moment: the ethics of conservations and sustainability.

Giving up omnipotence, which is closely linked to the civilisation of technical progress, must certainly lead to a "depressive" phase, in a Kleinian sense. However, this might probably be the *conditio sine qua non* for a decisive step towards greater individuation of the entire human species.

# Suspended cadence

The image that this book has opened up was a guitar being tuned.

In the background, as happens with a rhythm guitar, this same image has served as the titles of the various chapters, giving letters, words, and lines a musical flavour.

Now that the letters, words, and lines are coming to an end, we wish it to be with this image that the book reaches its conclusion.

The way in is also the way out, we have said.

In the foreground of the entire manuscript there has also been the other image, the ancient image of the *daídalon*, which emerged from the darkness of centuries to tell us once more about Possibility.

In the balance between destiny and history, between already trodden paths and ways to invent, between the certainty of death of the body and the longing for life of the soul ("intelligence independent from time and space", maintained a just over twenty-two-year-old Jung to his university classmates), the human being approaches the mystery of the Essence, making the journeys of their own personal Existence.

If the emergence of the consciousness from the unconscious over the history of the Psyche remains an enigma, in the individual history of each one of us, this has been partly illuminated by depth psychologies and the theories this has produced; indeed, which clinical practice has allowed them to produce.

From the opening chords, this book has posed the questions which have arisen in clinical experience, until the emergence of the main theme, the model of constellation of the archetype of Possibility seen as a powerful element of transformation both at individual and collective levels; moving then to the chorus of confrontation between the different means/models of describing something similar, and reaching the closing chords, which return possibility to its true meaning and deal with the issue of impossibility.

The finale, in this case, can only be a suspended chord, which does not resolve, as we would say in musical terms. The metaphor fits perfectly because, as we know, mysteries cannot be resolved. This also adapts well to expressing this sense of the unconcluded, which is not at all synonymous with inconclusive, as it can allow further issues to surface, as has been advocated from the start.

In the pages of this book, I have certainly expressed a topic which is close to me, typologically speaking, and have also tried to make clear the model that guides me in clinical practice. I have perceived in this model a plausible theory regarding the therapeutic factor, which would allow an insight into the practice of therapists from other schools too.

Then the topic became independent, as in musical improvisation, it looked at individuation and touched upon the negative in analysis, until making an incursion into the collective dimension, to try to understand where Western society is and where it could go.

The guitar ends on a suspended chord, to encourage this theme to be taken up once more by other instruments and other authors.

It is a chord that cannot be expressed in words, but which could gather around itself reflections and questions, just like when a guitar gathers unknown people around a fire on a summer's night, with the stars like tiny holes in a black velvet curtain, behind which there seems to be an intense light, in those unique moments between destiny and history, in which human beings sing, their eyes turned towards that silent labyrinth that is creation, hoping that that silence is listening.

# NOTES

## Chapter Two

1. "[…] Mith is the language of ambivalence; nothing is only this or that; the Gods and dancers will not stand still. They allow no sharp pictures of themselves, only visions" (Hillman, 1989, p. 37).
2. From the Akkadian *labirūte, laberūte*, said of kings and old buildings; also from *labirtu, labïru*, ancient.
3. The shape of the classical, curvilinear meandering labyrinth is very close to that of the spiral, an ancient and even more widespread symbol. In the early 900s, in Mesopotamia, clay tablets with spiral-shaped figures carved into them were found. The text in Babylonian cuneiform reveals that these tablets were a depiction of the entrails of animals offered up in sacrifice, like a sort of archive of the entrails of sacrificed animals. In fact, the original inscription makes reference to a "palace of entrails", from which academics came to recognise a representation of the Underworld. This world, visible in the assumed form of the internal organs of the animal, could be merciful or hostile to the world of the living, and it was therefore of the utmost importance to examine the entrails to discover the mood of the gods. The intestines were called *ekallu*, and this name refers to the Akkadian *ešgallu* or the "great temple of the underground world". Again, we have the image of the world of

the ancestors and the spiral-shaped version in which this is found, even among the Etruscans.

4. Similar dances were also performed at folklore events in Germany (for example, in fourteenth-century Münster) and in Switzerland. On an old painted vase, the François Vase of Florence, dancers are depicted standing in a row, and sitting facing them is Ariadne, as happened to the girl Hainuwele or the *jungfru* in the Scandinavian dances.

5. The Romans brought back use of the rope held by all the dancers in the so-called *Chorus Proserpinae*, as was done in the Greek dances. Livy himself speaks of a rope held between the hands of the dancers in a dance performed by the Queen of the Underworld, Persephone. Historians note that in the island of Delos the rope is mentioned as an essential element for the celebrations in honour of Britomartis, the Cretan equivalent of Artemis and a similar figure to Persephone. Artemis, Britomartis, Persephone, as well as Ariadne in Crete, are all feminine figures and goddesses who are related to death and rebirth.

6. Suggestively, even in a world far removed from Greece such as ancient China, there are labyrinth dances that are bird dances, for example the so-called "dance of Yü".

7. "[...] what does man express involuntarily through this movement, in dance and design? The same thing that germinal fluid produces in living things: eternal maintenance of life within death" (Kerényi, 1983, p. 70; translated for this edition).

8. Chronos, one of the oldest primitive gods in Greek mythology, is said to have been able to achieve intoxication by drinking only honey.

## Chapter Three

1. Mario Trevi (1924–2011) has been one of the first and more influential Jungian analysts in Italy.

2. "My justification for speaking of the existence of unconscious processes at all is derived simply and solely from experience, and in particular from psychopathological experience" (Jung, 1921/1971, p. 483).

3. Jung uses the term "archetype" for the first time in his work of 1919 entitled *Instinct and the Unconscious*, while in previous works he had expressed the same concept using the term "primordial image". He declares that the idea of an archetype came from the work of St. Augustine, while the term "archetype" can be found in Philo of Alexandria, in Dionysius the Areopagite, and in *Corpus Hermeticum*. Jung maintains that: "Archetypes are typical modes of apprehension, and wherever we meet with uniform and regularly recurring modes of

apprehension we are dealing with an archetype, no matter whether its mythological character is recognised or not. The collective unconscious consists of the sum of the instincts and their correlates, the archetypes" (Jung, 1919, pp. 137–138).

4. I have had the opportunity to hear described the pioneering studies on mirror neurons straight from Corrado Sinigaglia, one of the authors of the research, and it seemed clear to me that the neuron structures involved in the *action understanding* of which both apes and children under the age of three are capable, first of possessing conceivable processing ability, are something *a priori*, selected over millions of years of evolution, which make our brain able to organise certain experiences in a species-specific fashion.

5. As we know, not only did none of the children involved in the experiment develop any form of language but they also died.

6. In J. Knox (2003), *Archetype, Attachment, Analysis: Jungian Psychology and the Emergent Mind* (Hove: Brunner-Routledge). The author states similarly that "[The archetype is] a psychological feature arising out of the development of the human brain".

7. Dream three presented by Jung in his seminars on dreams, between 1928 and 1930, for example, shows the dreamer himself who sees a sort of labyrinth from above. Margaret Wilkinson, in a seminar held in Milan in 2007, presented the case of a patient who, using drawings over the course of analysis, depicted a woman and superimposed on her a classical labyrinth. It was an image drawn during an early stage of the analysis, and from our perspective it could have been considered very promising, representing the constellation of the *daídalon*.

## Chapter Four

1. With shaky theories on the archetypal content present in the psyche of a dog, we find ourselves in the company of Jung himself, when he writes: "There is nothing to prevent us from assuming that certain archetypes exist even in animals, that they are grounded in the peculiarities of the living organism itself" (Jung, 1917/1926/1943, p. 69).

2. Using the Greek name for the labyrinth, *daídalon*, to indicate the hypothetical construct proposed in this work, we do not wish to confuse the archetypal image with the archetype which may have generated it, but simply to give an evocative name to the latter.

3. Jung has the honour of being one of the first to call into question the medical model of psychotherapy in which, on one hand, there is the observed party, the patient, and on the other, the observer, the therapist, neutral and *super partes*.

4. Jung maintained, far ahead of his time, that "The great healing factor in psychotherapy is the doctor's personality, which is something not given at the start; it represents his performance at its highest and not a doctrinaire blueprint" (Jung, 1931, p. 88).

5. "The unconscious of the analyst, which feels and captures" refers to the topic of countertransference. Although the focus of this work is not to examine this concept, we might explore certain points in this respect.

The word "transference" indicates the *unconscious* transference by the patient of experience, patterns, relationships, emotions, and feelings related to reference figures onto the figure of the analyst, believed to be neutral and abstinent, a sort of "blank screen" or mirror.

Similarly, "countertransference" (or transference from the analyst) is initially defined as the *equally unconscious* transference onto the patient by the analyst of complexual aspects related to their own personal history.

This was considered to be a phenomenon that the analyst must quite rightly avoid, as it would hinder and contaminate the healing process. The emotions experienced by the analyst towards the patient (in particular, worryingly, erotic feelings) refer to the analyst's unanalysed content and the need to better handle their own complexual nodes. After a slow but gradual evolution in psychoanalytical thinking, nowadays the expressions "countertransference" or "countertransferal reactions" indicate any feeling, experience, emotion, thought, image, or sensation that the analyst experiences with regard to the patient.

It follows that we must try to distinguish whether and to what extent these are evoked by the patient, or rather provoked by their unconscious projections (which may thus reveal aspects regarding the functioning of the patient himself, unconscious content, complexes, and much more), or whether the patient is constellating the analyst's complexual aspects (and thus, if he becomes aware of this, the countertransference may reveal aspects belonging to the therapist and their psychic landscape).

Upon close examination, however, this distinction, which could be defined "work on countertransference", considered by many authors to be a factor in transformation and healing, reveals itself to be much more complex than the words make it appear, as transference and countertransference are the warp and woof of this unique and peculiar duet, created by the relationship between a patient and a therapist.

Projective identification of a patient who makes the therapist feel a certain way, would work in *that* way with *that* therapist, who, in turn, with his own personal equation, acts as a "hook", as Sedgwick puts it, for the projection of the patient. Work on countertransference, thus, speaks both of the unconscious content of the patient and of the analyst's "hook".

6. In reflection of this kind, today I would think that implicitly the patient perceives that I feel that there is a way out of their painful experiences, although they are yet to find it.

7. The italics are by the author of this book and highlight a key expression—"right to existence"—which could be seen also as "authorisation to exist" and is clearly related to "possibility/being able to exist".

8. "Every baby has his or her own favourable or unfavourable experience here. Dependence is maximal. The potential space happens only *in relation to a feeling of confidence* on the part of the baby, that is, confidence related to dependability of the mother-figure or environmental elements, confidence being the evidence of dependability that is becoming introjected" (Winnicott, 1971, p. 100; italics by Winnicott).

9. Given the relevance of what the author is expressing for the purposes of our discussion, I would like to quote *verbatim* what she indicated in the afterword: "For the patient, unable to relate to their Unconscious/Other, if their psyche is blocked by unilateralisation of neuroses, *thus a possibility is constellated*—not thought, but perhaps always sought, in its being avoided—to be exposed to the Unconscious, using (projection, projective identification, translation) the analyst as their own Unconscious" (Pessina, 2004, pp. 82–83; translated for this edition; italics added).

   And again: "The patient, especially serious patients, enter the setting, *unable* to conduct an intra-psychic relationship with their own Unconscious [...] In the setting/field, they have *the possibility* to begin to mobilise [...] The function of the analyst at this level is to provide a 'digestible' Unconscious (Guglieri, 2004) for the patient or a *possible* experience of the Other, which is in the end their own Unconscious [...] The analyst takes on the patient's unconscious through their intra-psychic capacity to re-elaborate their own unconscious infected by the patient [...] until it constellates, thanks to the Setting/field, with regard to the unconscious of the patient, a consciousness able to relate to it; constellating in itself, as in the Unconscious of the patient, a (*possible*) Consciousness of that unconscious" (Pessina, 2004, pp. 85–86; translated for this edition, italics added).

## Chapter Five

1. This and the following examples are translated for this edition from the book by M. Wuehl (2002), *Nella stanza dell'analista junghiano* (Milano: Vivarium). A text of this kind represents a valuable basis of comparison on the topic of therapeutic factors, and many other cases

described therein lend themselves to interpretation using the theory of constellation of the archetype of Possibility.

2. This is the case presented by Enrichetta Buchli. In a certain phase of analysis, the patient "dreams of entering a labyrinth-inferno, in which he would have stayed long, but from which he would have come out alive" (Buchli, in Wuehl, 2002, p. 321; translated for this edition).

On the one hand, this dream seems to anticipate the difficult period that awaited the patient, a period from which he effectively came out alive. On the other hand, it can represent the constellation of the *daídalon*. This shows the presence of psychic resources more vital than could be assumed from the patient's history.

In a later moment of great difficulty caused by the appearance of a serious form of cancer, the analyst, just as annihilated as the patient, manages to make a decisive intervention, in response to which the patient looks at her, listens, and the moment turns on itself, as if by some miracle. This is essentially an intervention in which the pain is shared, born together, "being with" it.

Furthermore, communication by the analyst of a highly evocative image for the patient allowed her to convey a sense of possibility, although in this case, it consisted essentially of accepting the inevitability of the situation, but seeing it with some symbolic meaning. The symbol allowed meaning to be given once more to what had appeared senseless, and to reactivate potential that appeared lost to the consciousness of both the patient and the analyst, but which clearly was not considered to be so in their unconscious.

3. This and the following statements are translated for this edition from the book by S. Bolognini (2000), *Il sogno cento anni dopo* (Torino, Bollati Boringhieri). The book contains the proceedings of a conference held by the Italian Psychoanalytical Society (SPI) in the centenary of Freud's *Traumdeutung*, written by a large group of Italian Freudian and neo-Freudian analysts.

4. "The dream recounted seems to contain a cry for help in order to construct (that) *the possibility to think* about aspects of mental life which are insufficiently developed and require *the presence of another to listen and understand* (can be constructed). In this respect, the dream recounted contains a reference not only to the unconscious but also to what cannot be represented mentally by the dreamer" (De Polo, in Bolognini, 2000, p. 80; translated for this edition, italics added).

5. In the words of Zucca Alessandrelli himself, all this is expressed in a very similar manner to our own: "For those who suffer from the grave condition of narcissism and dependence, being able to discover an authority which does not seek to dominate, nor demands obedience,

which does not seek to enslave, but proposes limits to a space in which to produce meaning with others, initially disconcerts, then provokes diffidence and aggression, and finally a *sense of possibility*. [GRF] promotes emergence and realisation of *an ability which is within* its members, even before the object-relationship" (*GRF: gruppo per la ripresa delle funzioni*, Gli Argonauti, n. 91, p. 335; translated for this edition, italics added).

6. This example is exposed in the note n. 2 in Jung (1920/1948, pp. 304–305).

7. Nathan deals with migrants from various places of origin in Africa or the Caribbean, living in France, even second or third generation, integrated into the Western mindset.

8. Let us consider the extreme case in which theory did not believe that the patient was treatable and consequently he was not treated, but merely isolated and hospitalised, as happened to psychotics for a good part of the twentieth century.

## Chapter Seven

1. "During the treatment of a psychotic individual, the most delicate, the most 'crucial' moment is when the patient becomes aware of his own inner space, a *space that offers* him *infinite possibilities*, but also appears as threatening and resistant to all domination. The patient wants *to get out* of himself and make contact with the other world; but when the delusional, megalomaniac outlook is deflated, he sees himself at the mercy of a persecutory experience. […] the external world appears full of dangers, which means that the patient may also develop an anxiety of an agoraphobic type. […] To cure means to pass from the terrain of illness, from pathological closedness, to another terrain, which is open and available, the world" (Resnik, 1987, p. 144; italics added).

2. The Swiss psychiatrist uses the Latin term indicating the mask worn by theatre actors, which serves the double purpose of assuming the identity of the character being played on stage, and amplifying the voice, making it audible for the audience in the theatre (*per sona*, through sounds). The idea of having to dissolve the Persona echoes a negative view, which does not sit well with the fact that it is a necessary and also positive psychic function.

3. In this way, we can fully understand the meaning of Trevi's words when he states that "The Individuation process does not have the naturalistic character of necessity, but rather the thoroughly human one of *possibility*; as such, it is subject to halts, inversions of meaning, partial

destructions and radical vanifications" (Trevi, in Aversa, 1995, p. 183; translated for this edition, italics added).

## Chapter Eight

1. As stated by Günther Anders (2003). To our greatest surprise, his fundamental reflections on the society of technology and its consequences on the psyche have not yet been translated into English.
2. Among many others, eloquent slogans such as "Impossible is nothing", "You can", "Just do it", "Life can be without walls", "No limits", come to mind.
3. In Italy, this has been for years a famous, and sadly misleading, advertisement of a mobile phone company.
4. We mainly refer to the interesting and challenging ideas which go by the name of "development of de-growth"; see the works by Serge Latouche.
5. Resizing the ego is not defined here as a reduction in value of the ego itself. The unconscious apparently needs an ego. The Self pre-disposes the birth of an ego; mysteriously, the essence seems to be embodied in existence. When I think of an ego that abandons its position in the centre of the psyche, I think of an ego which does however leave its own unique and unmistakeable imprint on the land. The land will be immeasurably vaster than the ego which runs through it, but it is the mark left by the footprint of the little ego that shapes it forever in a unique way.

# REFERENCES

Anders, G. (2003). *L'uomo è antiquato*, Vol. 1: *Considerazioni sull'anima nell'epoca della seconda rivoluzione industriale*. Torino: Bollati Boringhieri. [Anders, G. (1980). *Die Antiquiertheit des Menschen*, Band I: *Über die Seele im Zeitalter der zweiten industriellen Revolution*. München: Verlag C. H. Bech]

Anders, G. (2003). *L'uomo è antiquato*, Vol. 2: *Sulla distruzione della vita nell'epoca della terza rivoluzione industriale*. Torino: Bollati Boringhieri. [Anders, G. (1995). *Die Antiquiertheit des Menschen*, Band II: *Über die Zerstörung des Lebens im Zeitalter der dritten industriellen Revolution*. München: Verlag C. H. Bech]

Ariès, P. (1975). *Western Attitudes Towards Death: From the Middle Ages to the Present*. Baltimore, MD: The Johns Hopkins University Press.

Aversa, L. (1995). *Fondamenti di psicologia analitica*. Roma: Bari, Laterza.

Bauman, Z. (2003). *Liquid Love: On the Frailty of Human Bonds*. Cambridge: Polity Press.

Bauman, Z. (2007). *Liquid Times: Living in an Age of Uncertainty*. Cambridge: Polity Press.

Bolognini, S. (2000). *Il sogno cento anni dopo*. Torino: Bollati Boringhieri.

Brown, A. (1994). *Arthur Evans and the Palace of Minos*. Oxford: Ashmolean Museum.

Buber, M. (1965). *Knowledge of Man: A Philosophy of the Interhuman* (Ed. M. Friedman and Trans. M. Friedman & R. G. Smith). New York: Harper and Row.

Dürrenmatt, F. (1987). *Il Minotauro*. Milano: Marcos y marcos. [Dürrenmatt, F. (1985). *Minotaurus: Eine ballade*. Zürich: Diogenes Verlag]

Frey-Rohn, L. (1974). *From Freud to Jung: A Comparative Study of the Psychology of the Unconscious*. NY, G. P. Putnam's Sons for the C. G. Jung Foundation for Analytical Psychology.

Galimberti, U. (1997). Jung e la filosofia dell'Occidente. In: A. Carotenuto (a cura di), *Trattato di psicologia analitica*, vol. 1. Torino: Utet.

Galimberti, U. (1999). *Psiche e techne*. Milano: Feltrinelli.

Hillman, J. (1989). Senex and puer. In: *Puer Papers*. Dallas, TX: Spring.

Jung, C. G. (1908/1914). *The Content of the Psychoses*. In: *Collected Works*, vol. 3. Princeton, NJ: Bollingen Series XX, Princeton University Press.

Jung, C. G. (1916/1957). *The Transcendent Function*. In: *Collected Works*, vol. 8. Princeton, NJ: Bollingen Series XX, Princeton University Press.

Jung, C. G. (1917/1926/1943). *On the Psychology of the Unconscious*. In: *Collected Works*, vol. 7. Princeton, NJ: Bollingen Series XX, Princeton University Press.

Jung, C. G. (1920/1948). *The Psychological Foundations of Belief in Spirits*. In: *Collected Works*, vol. 8. Princeton, NJ: Bollingen Series XX, Princeton University Press.

Jung, C. G. (1921). *Definitions*. In: *Collected Works*, vol. 6. Princeton, NJ: Bollingen Series XX, Princeton University Press.

Jung, C. G. (1931). *The Aims of Psychotherapy*. In: *Collected Works*, vol. 16. London: Routledge & Kegan Paul.

Jung, C. G. (1934/1954). *Archetypes of the Collective Unconscious*. In: *Collected Works*, vol. 9. London: Routledge & Kegan Paul.

Jung, C. G. (1947/1954). *On the Nature of the Psyche*. In: *Collected Works*, vol. 8. Princeton, NJ: Bollingen Series XX, Princeton University Press.

Jung, C. G. (1957). *Collected Works*, vol. 1. London: Routledge & Kegan Paul.

Jung, C. G. (1966). *Collected Works*, vol. 15. London: Routledge & Kegan Paul.

Jung, C. G. (1967). *Collected Works*, vol. 4. London: Routledge & Kegan Paul.

Jung, C. G. (1969). *Collected Works*, vol. 11. London: Routledge & Kegan Paul.

Jung, C. G. (1973). *Collected Works*, vol. 2. London: Routledge & Kegan Paul.

Kalsched, D. (1996). *The Inner World of Trauma: Archetypal Defenses of the Personal Spirit*. London: Routledge.

Kalsched, D. E. (2012). *Trauma and the Soul: A Psycho-Spiritual Approach to Human Development and Its Interruption*. London: Routledge.

Kast, V. (1992). *The Dynamics of Symbols: Fundamentals of Jungian Psychotherapy*. New York: Fromm.

Kerényi, K. (1983). *Nel labirinto*. Torino: Bollati Boringhieri.

[This collection of essays, entitled *"Nel labirinto"* does not exist in any other language but Italian, not even in German. The original papers we refer to are:

Kerényi, K. (1941). *Labyrinth-Studien: Labyrinthos als Linienreflex einer mmythologischen Idee*. In: *Albae Vigiliae*, vol. 15. Amsterdam and Lipsia: Pantheon.

Kerényi, K. (1956). *Die Herrin des Labyrinthes*. In: *Neue Zürcher Zeitung*, 25 October]

Kerényi, K. (1963). *Vom Labyrinthos zum Syrthos: Gedanken über den griechischen Tanz*. In: *Atlantis*, vol. 35.

Kerenyi, K., & Jung, C. G. (1969). *Essay on a Science of Mythology: The Myth of the Divine Child*. Princeton, NJ: Princeton University Press.

Nathan, T. (1996). *Principi di etnopsicoanalisi*. Torino: Bollati Boringhieri.

[Nathan, T. (1993). *Fier de n'avoir ni pays ni amis, quelle sottise c'était ... Principes d'ethnopsycanalyse*. Grenoble: Éditions La Pensèe Sauvage]

Nathan, T. (2003). *Non siamo soli al mondo*. Torino: Bollati Boringhieri.

[Nathan T. (2001). *Nous ne sommes pas seuls au monde*, Paris, Les Empêcheurs de penser en rond]

Nathan, T., & Stengers, I. (1996). *Medici e stregoni*. Torino: Bollati Boringhieri.

[Nathan, T., & Stengers, I. (1995). *Médecin et sorciers: Manifeste pour une psychopathologie scientifique, Le médicin et le charlatan*. Paris: Les Empêcheurs de penser en rond]

Pessina, M. M. (2004). *Simbolo, affetto e oltre ...* Milano: Vivarium.

Resnik, S. (1987). *The Theatre of the Dream*. London: Tavistock.

Sedgwick, D. (1994). *The Wounded Healer: Countertransference from a Jungian Perspective*. London: Routledge.

Seligman, M. (2011). *Learned Optimism*. Australia: Heinemann.

Tagliacozzo, R. (1992). *Il sogno: progetto vitale e progetto psicoanalitico*, relazione al Centro Milanese di Psicoanalisi.

Trevi, M. (1987). *Per uno junghismo critico*. Milano: Studi Bompiani.

Trevi, M. (1991). *Adesione e distanza. Una lettura critica de "L'Io e l'inconscio" di Jung*. Roma: Melusina.

Winnicott, D. W. (1971). *Playing and Reality*. London: Tavistock.

Winnicott, D. W. (1977). *Through Paediatrics to Psycho-Analysis*. London: Hogarth.

Wuehl, M. (2002). *Nella stanza dell'analista junghiano*. Milano: Vivarium.

Zoja, L. (1995). *Growth and Guilt: Psychology and the Limits of Development*. London: Routledge.

Zucca Alessandrelli, C. (2001–2002). *GRF: gruppo per la ripresa delle funzioni*, Gli Argonauti, nr. 91–92. Milano: CIS editore.

# INDEX

active protagonist 30
*aliquid stat pro aliquot* 22
Anders, G. ix
antilibidinal ego 72
archetypes 59, 82
    *daídalon* 42
    defined 27
    metastoric aspect 27
    possibility 71, 84
Ariès, P. 89
Aversa, L. 108

Bauman, Z. 94
Bolognini, S. 54, 106
Brown, A. 12
Buber, M. xvii
Buondelmonti, Cristoforo 12

cave of the Sibyl 13
cave paintings 15
Chiesa, Susanna 49

Chomsky, Noam 26
civilised society 87
classical labyrinth xv, 14–16,
    28–30, 103
*Collected Works* (Jung) 57
collective unconscious 24–25, 38,
    103
conscious(ness) xiv, xxi–xxii, 6, 21–22,
    24–25, 27, 36, 38–39, 44–45,
    47, 50, 52–53, 55, 57–58, 63,
    69–73, 75, 79–85, 87, 89,
    92–94, 97, 99, 105–106
    self- 68
conscious–unconscious system 38
*The Content of the Psychoses* (Jung) 4
"corresponding chord" 24
countertransferal fantasy 50
countertransferal reactions 6, 104
Cretan
    civilization 12
    coins 14

*daídalon* 12
  labyrinth 13, 67
  palace temple 19
Crete 11–13, 18, 29, 102

Dante's dark forest 5
"defences of the self" 72
*dementia praecox* 4
destructive polarity 67
"developing" societies 58
dialectical process 38
dream process 54
dual-compartment box 36
Dürrenmatt, F. 67–90

ego 24, 27, 30, 39, 45–46, 50–51, 57,
        71–72, 75, 77, 80–81, 96–97,
        108
ego complex xxi, 8, 44–46, 52, 71, 77,
        81–84
ego development xiv
e-motion 39
enigma 52, 58, 99
ethno-psychoanalysis 56
Evans, Arthur 12

Fairbairn's "internal saboteur" 72
feeling-toned complexes 24,
        27, 83
Franciosi, Elisabetta 51
Frey-Rohn, L. 4, 37

Galimberti, U. 23, 86, 89
Gorer, Geoffrey 91
gradient 37–39
Greek civilization 19
GRF (Group for the Recovery of
        Functions) 55
guitar
    tuning 4
    "A" 3
Guntrip's "antilibidinal ego" 72

hermeneutics 22
Hillman, J. 11, 101
*hodos* 5

*In the Labyrinth* (Kerényi) 9
individuation process 80

Jung, C. G. ix, xiii, xv, xvii, xix,
        xxi–xxii, xxv–xxvi, 4, 6, 9,
        19, 21–22, 24, 26–27, 30–31,
        37–39, 44, 50, 52, 54, 57–58,
        71, 80–84, 92, 94, 99, 102–104
Jungian theory of opposites 67

Kalsched, D. ix, xv–xvi, 6, 72–73
Kast, V. ix, xiv, 44–45
Kerényi, K. xv, xx, 9, 12–13, 15, 17–19,
        23, 28, 72, 102
Kingdom of the Dead 13

*labrys* 12–13, 17, 29
labyrinth, symbol of 28, 30, 101
"labyrinth of the psychic discomfort"
        53
*labyrinthos* 12–13
Lady of the Labyrinth 18

Malta 15
*Maro* Indonesian rite dance 30
megalithic cultures 15
*metà* 5
*metà-hodos* 5
Minoan civilization 12
Minos, King 9, 12, 17–18, 29, 68
Minotaur xv–xvi, 9, 12, 16, 18, 29,
        67–71, 96

Nathan, T. 56–58, 107
negative therapeutic reaction 67
neolithic cultures 15

*Opus* 80, 84

perception of a possibility
46, 76
Pessina, M. M. 46–47, 105
place of ancestors 13
placebo effect 55, 58
possibility 21, 28, 35, 67
concept 30
inklings 53
possibility of meaning 51
prophetic dreams 53
psychic energy 51
psychic process 63
psychotics 4, 77, 107
"pushed down" 41

realised possibility 29
Resnik, S. 77, 107
rigid theory 63

Sandplay Therapy 59
"savage" societies 56
schizophrenics 4
Sedgwick, D. 104
Seinfeld's "bad object" 72
Seligman, M. 35–36
"society of eternal youth" 92
Stengers, I. 56
symbol 23–24, 50, 57, 59, 80,
83–84, 106

Tagliacozzo, R. 54
terrible psychic inflations 97
tertium non datur 22
theories of the psyche 31
theory of the mind 63
Titanic 97
transcendent function 22, 46–47, 50,
80, 83
Trevi, M. 21, 25, 28, 102, 107–108

unconscious xiv–xv, xxi, xxvi, 6, 19,
21, 24–31, 36–39, 42, 44–47,
50, 52–55, 57–59, 63, 68–73,
75–77, 79–85, 92–93, 96–97,
99, 102–106, 108
collective 24–25, 38, 103
"unmodifiability" of archetypal
content 73

web
electromagnetic waves 94
internet 94
Western culture 56
Western society 85
Winnicott, D. W. 45–46, 53, 105
Wuehl, M. 50–51, 105–106

Zoja, L. x, 93
Zucca Alessandrelli, C. 55, 106